AGAINST ALL ODDS

HOW PATSIE CAMPANA ROSE FROM THE DEPTHS OF THE SEA TO THE HEIGHTS OF INDUSTRY

— *The Campana Family* —
WITH DENNIS SEEDS

SMART BUSINESS® BOOKS
An Imprint of Smart Business® Network Inc.

Against all Odds
Copyright © 2018 by The Campana Family

All rights are reserved.

No part of this publication may be reproduced, distributed or transmitted in any form or by any means, including photocopying, recording or other digital or mechanical methods, without the prior written permission of the author, except in the cases of fair use as permitted by U.S. and international copyright laws. For permission requests, please submit in writing to the publisher at the address below:

Published by:
Smart Business Network
835 Sharon Drive, Suite 200
Westlake, OH 44145

Printed in the United States of America
Editor: Dustin S. Klein

ISBN: 978-1-945389-63-4
Library of Congress Control Number: 2018950971

Printed in USA

TABLE OF CONTENTS

PART ONE
THE EARLY YEARS 1

CHAPTER 1
AN INQUISITIVE YOUTH WITH LOVING PARENTS 3

CHAPTER 2
PROUDLY SERVING IN WORLD WAR II 17

CHAPTER 3
HOME FROM THE WAR... AS LOVE BLOSSOMS 33

PART TWO
BUILDING A FAMILY AND
BECOMING A BUSINESSMAN 47

CHAPTER 4
FINDING A NICHE IN THE BUSINESS WORLD 49

CHAPTER 5
HOME AND AWAY:
A LETTER WRITER SHARES DEEP THOUGHTS 57

CHAPTER 6
AN INVENTOR AT HEART 73

CHAPTER 7
CROSSED PATHS: HOW A RELATIONSHIP
WITH A VETERAN STEEL EXECUTIVE LED TO
SUCCESSFUL BUSINESS VENTURES 89

PART THREE
PATSIE, THE MAN 103

CHAPTER 8
VICTORIES OVER HEALTH ISSUES 105

TABLE OF CONTENTS

CHAPTER 9
A SECRET PHILANTHROPIST 111

CHAPTER 10
THE SPECIAL FRIENDSHIP 119

CHAPTER 11
NOVEMBER 24, 1993:
THE DAY PATSIE WAS CALLED HOME... 129

PART FOUR
THE NEXT GENERATION... 141

CHAPTER 12
THE TORCH IS PASSED TO OTHERS
IN THE CAMPANA FAMILY.. 143

CHAPTER 13
THE CAMPANA FAMILY DIVERSIFIES 147

PART FIVE
REFLECTIONS & ANECDOTES
BY LOVED ONES AND FRIENDS 155

CHAPTER 14
STORIES ABOUT THE MAN
UNDERSCORE HIS LIFE... AND LEGEND 157

EPILOGUE 181

INTRODUCTION

Of the more than four million Italian immigrants who had arrived in America by 1924, what are the chances that one would rise from those humble beginnings to become a U.S. Navy war hero, provide for a loving family by founding a business (which would grow into a multimillion-dollar enterprise), and sacrifice his own personal interests so others would benefit from his success and anonymous generosity?

Patsie C. Campana Sr. would go on to do all those things, and more. He beat the odds because he did it his way. This is his story.

An avid reader, Patsie was a non-stop learner, hard worker, and positive thinker. He was an opportunist, risk-taker, patent holder, and the ultimate team player. Patsie was a teacher, leader, and an effective communicator. He was a patriot, a decorated Navy deep sea diver, and a mentor. Beyond that, Patsie was a master mechanic, an expert welder, electrician, and an engineer. He also held dozens of patents; demonstrating through actions rather than words his innovation, focus, and persistence.

Patsie was a friend and a grandfather. He was a father and husband. And for 47 years, he was the soulmate of his wife, Jeneé.

While complex, Patsie was also simple: He was quick to say "please," "thank you," "that was a first-class job," "I appreciate your effort," "you earned and deserved this," and "congratulations."

Passionate and fun, he was also strict and intense. He was fair and honest, loyal and compassionate, loving and happy. While Patsie was successful, he was also lucky. Along the way, he had help from a lot of people—many loyal employees and business partners, friends, and family. Patsie was a friend to the kings of industry, as well as the common laborer. If you saw him and did not know him, you would think he was the epitome of "everyman."

From his earliest days, Patsie was inquisitive. Once he discovered what made something tick, he challenged himself to discover how to make it tick more efficiently. It was this intellectual curiosity which defined Patsie's approach to business. As you read his story, you will learn there was never a challenge from which Patsie shied away. Those who knew and loved him offer their stories of—and insight into—what made him such a unique and special individual who was beloved by so many people.

The challenges that Patsie faced—and overcame—began at an early age. When he was about five years old, he was injured in a near-fatal circus wagon accident.

Later, during World War II, Patsie became a Navy diver and risked his life in 1,200 hours of repairs and recovery efforts under water. He put in relentless effort as an innovator; inventing or improving both processes and products to help his country.

But perhaps the greatest challenge of all was when, at age 48, he gave up a successful vice president position at a large electrical construction company to found his own business. Over the years—and against the odds—Patsie grew this company into a multi-million-dollar enterprise and employed, at its peak, more than 1,000 employees in Lorain County, Ohio, and across the country.

Beyond his business acumen, Patsie was dedicated to giving back to others. He was generous to so many people and organizations, yet he didn't want credit for his good deeds. As a testament to that philosophy, he raised his children to be givers as well. To this day, they have perpetuated his legacy.

We hope as you read about the life of Patsie C. Campana Sr. that you are inspired to follow your own dreams, find courage in your actions, and not let the word "failure" become part of your vocabulary.

—The Campana Family
July, 2018

Larry, Patsie, Thomas, Albert, Maria and Baldo, circa 1930.

PART ONE

THE EARLY YEARS

CHAPTER 1

AN INQUISITIVE YOUTH WITH LOVING PARENTS

The circus parade wound its way down Lorain's Washington Avenue as young Pasquale Carmen Campana sat on the curb in front of his family's market and excitedly watched the procession. He was five years old.

Patsie, Larry and Baldo, circa 1926.

The Campana Family, circa 1925.

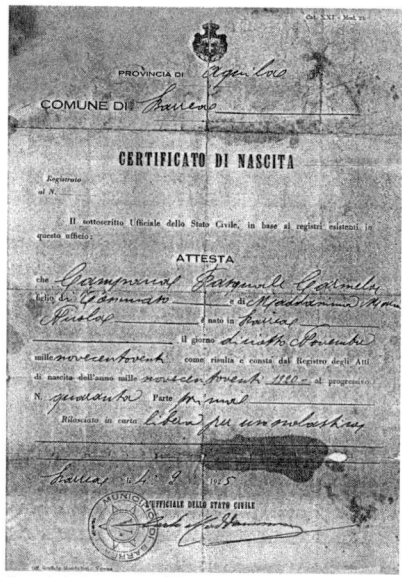

Patsie's birth certificate.

Having been born in 1920 in Barrea, Italy, this was the first time Pasquale experienced this type of spectacle, with so many amazing sights and sounds. He was mesmerized by the pageantry.

The Campana Café was location on Washington Avenue in Lorain.

Thomas and Maria Nicole Campana, Pasquale's parents, worked hard to establish their lives in the United States. They emigrated to Lorain in 1922. Within a few years, they opened a small shop—Campana's Market—at 1850 Washington Street. Thomas doubled as a butcher

CHAPTER 1

and sold grocery goods to neighborhood families. He had completed the building around 1926 and subsequently added a small café. The growing structure kept growing, eventually consisting of the Campana family home, three apartments, and the market/cafe.

For Pasquale, whom people called "Patsie", the parade was magical. He needed a close-up look.

The youth squirmed away from his parents and dashed into the street. In the commotion, he fell under the wheels of a heavily laden circus wagon. Patsie could have easily been killed, but he wasn't. Instead, he survived and was badly injured. The wheels fractured his skull, broke both legs, and one arm.

Shocked, Thomas and Maria rushed into the street themselves, scooped up their son, and rushed him to St. Joseph Hospital. Doctors set his broken bones and placed a wooden clamp device on his head to allow the depressed skull fracture to heal. Later, Patsie would develop a bulging vein from the trauma to his forehead. The vein often flared whenever his blood pressure increased, due to excitement or stress. It looked like a "V," or a backwards 2.

The initial 48 hours after the accident were a critical time. Patsie had survived the impact of the injuries, but doctors paid close attention to him until that period of time had passed. Then, he settled in to a long recovery that would continue to remain touch and go for a long time.

Patsie's convalescence took priority for the family, which also included his younger brothers—Larry, 2, and Baldo, an infant. In the years after the accident, the brothers gained two more siblings—Albert, in 1929, and Rosemary, in 1934.

As Patsie's lengthy recovery began, Thomas and Maria wanted to keep an eye on him as they worked. They brought him to the shop each day and placed him on a stool behind the candy counter—and subsequently put him to work, or at least as much work as a youth recovering from terrible injuries could do. Patsie cut chocolate into small chunks and sold lollipops, which cost a penny each (smaller ones were two-for-a-penny).

AGAINST ALL ODDS / THE PATSIE CAMPANA STORY

The Campana Market was a neighborhood fixture.

By age 13, Patsie was working regularly in the family's new business—a tavern. Prohibition had been repealed in 1933, and Thomas quickly obtained a liquor license for his café. The café was one of the first in Lorain to become a tavern after the federal ban on liquor was lifted. And so, by the time he was 16 years old, Patsie was "pushin' beer" to thirsty customers.

In the 1930s, Lorain was a bustling city. With several large industries based there, it attracted a wide variety of immigrants—Poles, Italians, Czechs, Romanians, Greeks, and Germans—who sought work in the factories. Altogether, there were more than 55 different nationalities represented in Lorain. Many of them became "regulars" at the tavern. It was truly a melting pot that defined America at that time.

Tomasso and Maria with a bottle of vino.

CHAPTER 1

Patsie's mother, Maria, was just as committed to the family business as her husband. For example, she would garden on very hot days while Thomas tended bar. Every couple of hours or so, he would take a break from bartending and she would take a break from gardening and come inside.

Knowing how hot it became in the tavern, Maria would go outside with Thomas and help cool down her husband. She would stand on a Cotton Club Soda wooden box because she was so short. There, she would remove Thomas' customary short sleeve, white button-down shirt, take a sponge that had been soaking in ice water, and wipe Thomas to cool him off. Then, she would replace his shirt with one that was drying on the clothes line, and Thomas would return to tending bar. And, a few hours later, Maria would be ready to cool Thomas off the next time he needed it. It was truly a family affair.

Like the tavern, the Campana home was a hub of activity in the heavily populated Italian neighborhood. Early on, the market and café unfortunately drew attention from the Mob. A few enforcers approached Thomas and "asked" him to pay insurance protection money. Thomas refused—he had an ace in the hole: contacts in Sicily, where the Mob was centered.

Thomas sent word to the right people back at home, and the enforcers backed off their pressure on the former Carabiniere. Despite this, street gangs formed in the neighborhood. Fighting was common.

Growing up, Patsie was no angel. But he kept his nose clean.

"I could have belonged to any of those gangs, and I was pretty well accepted," he told a Lorain Journal reporter in a 1973 feature story. "But I was always the small guy, so I usually carried a stick…"

In spite of the circus parade accident, Patsie's inquisitive nature remained one of his greatest traits. Every day, on his way to school, he passed by a workshop that intrigued him—there were frequent colored flashes and smoke visible through the windows. Part of the reason it interested him so much was that he didn't know what was happening there… and he had to find out.

AGAINST ALL ODDS / THE PATSIE CAMPANA STORY

PATSIE'S ITALIAN ORIGINS AND HIS HANDS-ON PARENTS

Vintage postcard showing Barrea in the 1920s.

Patsie's mother and father were from the Abruzzo region of mid-southern Italy, specifically the village of Barrea in the province of L'Aquila. Their last name, Campana, meant "bell." The people of Barrea were inclined to be self-employed, most often in the engineering, construction, and artisan fields. Among the villagers, there was a remarkable amount of parental pride in having one's offspring become a successful entrepreneur.

Tomasso Campana in his Carabiniere uniform, circa 1913.

Tomasso (Thomas) Campana, Patsie's father, was a man of many talents. With only a fourth-grade education, he was a tough six-footer with a distinguished career as a federal police officer in Italy—a Carabiniere—who received a European Carnegie Hero medal for his bravery in saving lives.

Maria Nicole Maddamma was a little over five feet tall, but she could tackle any chore—from preparing the finest Italian food around, to pouring concrete and repairing the plumbing.

As far as size goes, Patsie would be a blend of both his parents. He would grow to be 5'7."

CHAPTER 1

Thomas first came to America in 1905 at the age of 15 and was accompanied by Sabatino, his brother. Sabatino was already settled in the United States, arriving in Lorain, Ohio in 1902.

After several years in Lorain, Thomas returned to Italy and in 1912 became a Carabiniere, the Italian national police force. One of his first feats was to win a silver medal for long-distance running in the Royal Italian Army Gymnastics Competition in Rome on December 19, 1912.

Within a few years, he distinguished himself for his heroism: In 1915, he helped rescue victims following an earthquake that destroyed the village of Avezzano, receiving the bronze Carnegie Medal. More than 30,000 people were killed in the disaster.

A fire had trapped college students on a second-floor building; the balcony doors were locked, and there was no way to safety. Thomas tied a rope around a rock, threw it onto the balcony and snagged a safe hold. He climbed the rope, broke open the doors, and led the students and others to safety.

He was later transferred to Rome. Thomas' next position was given to him by King Victor Emmanuel III. He became a bodyguard and nanny for the king's son, Prince Umberto, and served in that role for several years at the royal palace in Rome.

While serving with the Carabinieri in World War I, Thomas was hit with mustard gas. After being hospitalized, he eventually recovered. He later received

The prestigious Carnegie Medal was awarded to Tomasso, along with other medals.

Tomasso became a Carabineri on foot patrol in 1912.

continued on page 10

continued from page 9

La Medaglia a Ricordo Della Guerra Europea, a World War I victory medal. Following the war, the political climate in Italy changed. The Fascists rose to power. Thomas met Maria in Barrea during these uncertain times, and the two were married shortly after the war ended.

They heard about opportunities in America. Hoping for a safer environment for his family, Thomas on October 7, 1920, went back to Lorain, Ohio, to prepare for married life with Maria, who was about to give birth. On November 17, 1920, their son was born and was named after Thomas' father Pasquale Campana. For nearly two years, Maria remained in Barrea raising Pasquale while Thomas was in Lorain.

After World War I, Thomas Campana received this service award.

By 1922, Thomas' hard work had paid off. He had earned enough money for Maria and Pasquale to join him at 1027 W. 18th Street, Lorain. Along with $40, Maria arrived in September that year with her courage, excitement, and determination to find the American dream.

Sunday dinners at the Campanas were a time of family togetherness. Pictured are Rosemary, Maria, Thomas, Albert, his wife Alberta, and Patsie.

Maria Nicole Campana was just as hard a worker as her husband. She cooked for the café, and supported her husband and family in any way she could. She was an unofficial consultant for newly-immigrated Italian families, and became very involved with St. Peter's Catholic Church on West 17th Street—just a few blocks from their home.

CHAPTER 1

There was Italian wedding soup, garlic soup, pasta, pizza, calzones, sausage and peppers, and the best Italian cheeseburger in town, with fresh salami and provolone cheese.

Often, in pure Italian family tradition, Thomas would sit under a grape arbor in the back yard and play his mandolin or guitar as family and friends gathered around. There was singing and happiness, an occasional glass of homemade wine, and everyone shared the simple things in life with those they loved.

The Campana family: Maria, Albert, Tomasso, Rosemary, Patsie and Baldo.

Eventually, Patsie went inside and introduced himself to the owner. He told him he often walked by, and asked if the owner would show him what all the activity was about.

"Well, we do welding," the owner explained, and showed Patsie some of the equipment.

As the conversation continued, the two bonded. Patsie offered to help in the shop. In return, the owner offered to teach him about welding. This then became one of those rare, chance meetings—one which set Patsie on a career journey by sparking an interest in welding and the use of metals.

It didn't take long before Patsie's incessant search for knowledge made him an avid reader with a hunger to learn. His father recognized his abilities and encouraged him to pursue his interests and find work in Lorain's steel industry. This was yet another instance where Patsie succeeded against the odds; had his recovery from the injuries not been so complete, he likely would not have been able to pursue manual labor work.

HOW "PASQUALE" GOT THE NICKNAME "PATSIE"

A Harrison Elementary School teacher named Ethel M. Dolbear decided that "Patsie" was easier for young Pasquale Carmen Campana to spell and for her to remember. The name stuck. Patsie initially spoke only the patois dialect spoken in Barrea and couldn't understand English. As a result, he had to repeat the first grade.

Failure was not something Patsie accepted. He learned English, and with his ever-present curiosity and resourcefulness, went on to be successful in school with a better ability to focus on learning.

Patsie's high school graduation photo. Lorain High School class of 1940 A.

On occasion, unfamiliar people mistook "Patsie" for a girl's name. The Polk's City Directory of Lorain for 1939 lists him as "Patsy, student." While enumerator Catherine Samaka was taking the 1940 Census, she wrote down "Betsy – daughter" for 19-year-old Patsie after she interviewed Patsie's mother, Maria.

Then, when the papers were filed in 1963 for one of Patsie's early patents—a traffic signal pre-emption device for emergency vehicles—his name was inadvertently spelled "Patsy."

To most, however, he was "Patsie," or an occasional "P.C."

Long-time accountant John Zalick recalls him saying, "Don't call me Mr. Campana; just call me Patsie."

His wife Jeneé, though, simply called him "Pat."

Patsie followed his father's advice and soon became a valuable employee at the American Ship Building Co., one of the largest employers in Lorain. There, Patsie led a team that bent shell plates for the sides of a ship. He discovered he had a real talent for laying them out and bending them—which would end up serving him well.

At the time, workers were paid for this type of work by the piece. That meant a lot of money during war time. For example, in 1941, when

CHAPTER 1

MARIA PLAYS A ROLE IN DELAYING THE STORK

Patsie's brother Larry unfortunately was killed September 1, 1944, while serving in France. It was a sad turn of events that deeply affected Patsie, and of course, his family. Patsie's third child, a son, was named in honor of his brother.

But it was not that simple. While Maria Campana wanted her grandson named after her son, Larry, who was killed in World War II, she was adamant about the timing.

Patsie's third child was supposed to be born on August 9, 1953. But grandmother Maria told Patsie and his wife, Jeneé, that it would be impossible for the boy to be named after Larry unless the child was born after the anniversary of his death, September 1.

"My due date's a month earlier than that," Jeneé told her.

Maria replied, "If he's born any sooner than that, he can't be named after my son."

The days came and went. The baby was born on September 2.

Well... her children always said Maria Campana had some strange ways.

Larry Campana's high school graduation photo.

Patsie and his mother Maria, circa 1940.

he was 21, Patsie earned $14,000. The average salary at the time was $956 a year, so this was excellent money.

Because he worked for American Ship Building Co., which was a defense contractor, Patsie received military deferments from active service. He was given one deferment from military service every six months. This happened six consecutive times—until Patsie decided to enlist in the U.S. Navy.

13

Not only was being deferred during WWII viewed as a little unusual, the situation made Patsie a bit envious of his brothers and friends who were in the service and doing their patriotic duty.

Campana Family 1930

Patsie's brother Baldo, 18, was the first Campana sibling to enlist. Larry, 20, had been deferred for medical reasons (a high-arched foot), but wanted to join the military as well.

Patsie tried to talk him out of it, but Larry didn't listen. The two last saw each other during an argument over enlisting: "What, are you nuts? You've got to stay out of the war," Patsie told him.

But Larry was determined; on May 10, 1943, he joined the Army, leaving Patsie the sole "holdout."

By January 1944, Patsie had enough. He had received his seventh deferment, and he didn't want it.

"I can't accept this," he said. "I have a brother in France, and I have one in India; I'm the oldest of all my brothers, and I have to go."

On January 24, 1944, Patsie enlisted.

When he reported for duty in Tacoma, Washington, it began another chapter in his life—one which would be marked by amazing feats of heroism and outstanding completion of duties. It would also mark yet another instance where Pastie overcame the odds to succeed—although in this case, it meant survive.

CHAPTER 1

Patsie's time in the armed forces also led to yet another chance encounter—this time with his future wife, Dolores Jean Hume (better known as Jeneé).

The two met in a ballroom, where hundreds of servicemen met hundreds of girls. It was a case of love at first sight. Their love blossomed into a lifetime romance that never waned.

CHAPTER 2

PROUDLY SERVING IN WORLD WAR II

Patsie was anxious to get to work when he joined the Navy. It was his nature to jump with both feet into whatever he was doing, and the Navy was a logical choice for service because of Patsie's shipbuilding experience. But, he soon discovered that building a ship and serving on it were two different things. There was much Patsie had to learn about military service, but like his brothers before him, he was up to the challenge.

He reported to Navy Boot Camp at Naval Station Great Lakes, near Chicago, for six weeks of Boot Camp. This was a completely different adventure for Patsie, and he would need to rely on his wits and ability to persevere to complete his training.

After Boot Camp, Patsie was assigned to the U.S.S. *Hamlin*, a new ship that was being built in Tacoma, Washington. Because of his shipbuilding experience, Patsie was named a shipfitter third class. He later advanced his rank to first class. Shipfitters kept the craft in ship-shape and were trained in patching leaks and repairing damages.

In what was probably an event beyond his control, Patsie met his future mother-in-law before he met his future wife: Edna Hume and her husband David worked at Todd-Pacific Shipyards, where the U.S.S. *Hamlin* was being built. David was a shipbuilder, and Edna a pipefitter.

One morning, there was a challenge thrown down: that a short-but-strong sailor named Patsie could move a heavy box of rivets. Edna

NAVY BOOT CAMP BROUGHT DISCIPLINE

A picture of what Navy Boot Camp was like for Patsie Campana, and tens of thousands of other Navy enlistees, is no further away than a memoir by Navy officer William J. Veigele called "Sea Bag of Memories."

Veigele trained at the same Boot Camp as Patsie, the Naval Station Great Lakes, near Chicago, several months before Patsie arrived. The follow includes excerpts from Veigele's descriptions.

Once a recruit got his shots and a buzz cut, he got rid of his civilian clothes and possessions. He shipped them home, and then, standing in his birthday suit with hundreds of other recruits, he received Navy-issued uniforms as Navy supply clerks tossed out clothes and other gear he would use during his service.

Patsie enlisted in the U.S. Navy, where he made a name for himself.

There was little attention to clothing size, so every crewman had to learn the proper way to wear them—and accept the potentially ill-fitting clothes. The Navy then issued Patsie his sleeping gear; it was tradition to issue a hammock with a mattress, two mattress covers, a pillow, two pillow cases and two blankets. These were all to be stored in a Sea Bag.

The Sea Bag was a canvas sack, about 26 by 36 inches. It had a draw string so it could be closed and hung on a peg. As with everything else the recruit got, he stenciled his name on the side of the bag—it had everything he owned in it, and was his entire and unique identity as an individual among the mass of other men.

Before rolling his mattress into the sack, a sailor positioned his bedding items on the flattened mattress. It had to be prepared first according to regulations and then inserted in a certain order. This procedure ensured first that the clothing would take up a minimum of space. Secondly, by rolling items, they tended to have fewer wrinkles when unrolled.

CHAPTER 2

Then the Navy issued the recruit his "bible," The Bluejackets' Manual, which contained all the material the recruit would need to know to become a sailor and handle himself accordingly at his future stations, ashore or afloat.

The training program in Boot Camp featured commands such as, "Up and at 'em," "Drop 'em and grab 'em," "Fire drill," "Scrub down that deck," "Inspection," "Move it, Boot," and "Now, I ain't your mommy asking you. It's me. I'm telling you." The chief petty officer assigned to a Boot Camp company shouted these commands mostly in the middle of the night after a difficult and tiring 10-hour day of marching, calisthenics, scrubbing clothes, rifle-over-your-head drills, pulling oars in a boat, loading heavy shells in a five-inch gun and other training activities. The harassment was designed to get the recruits accustomed to discipline, to respond to disagreeable orders, and to function with only a few hours of sleep.

When a recruit graduated from Boot Camp, he became a new sailor. Proudly, and with a grunt because of its weight, he swung up his Sea Bag and balanced it on his shoulder. He marched off to his first leave and his assignment. Aboard ship, he moved the contents of his Sea Bag into a locker. Now he no longer felt or thought like a recruit. He was a sailor and would start his cruise with the Navy.

decided to bet on him—and won the pot. So, not only was he her hero for the moment, but she took a liking to the affable Patsie. Little did she know that her daughter would soon bring Patsie into the family.

The U.S.S. Hamlin.

In June 1944, the U.S.S. *Hamlin* was commissioned. She set off on her shakedown cruise, stopping at San Francisco and San Pedro.

Patsie was now one of the *Hamlin*'s plank owners (a Navy term for a member of a ship's first crew). This was an exciting time for everyone on board, and the shakedown cruise was later described by the ship's chaplain, Samuel Hill Ray, S.J., in a journal he wrote after the war:

> *The commissioning of a ship is a thrill. The riveting, painting and hammering days are over. You have watched your future home take shape. You know with a secret hope that your safety is tied up with hers. Finally, the ship is under her own steam and after a run out into the harbor, she comes alongside the dock and the crew moves aboard. We are actually living in the U.S.S. Hamlin, built in the Todd Ship Yards in Tacoma, Washington.*
>
> *On June 26, 1944, at 1400, the program of commissioning began. Guests were seated above the seaplane deck and all hands assembled on the seaplane deck itself. Captain*

CHAPTER 2

HOW PATSIE AND JENEÉ MET AMONG THE HUNDREDS IN A TACOMA BALLROOM

Patsie was earning a reputation with his feats of strength while the U.S.S. *Hamlin* was in port, but it was when he was off-duty that a teenage girl in a Tacoma dance hall would sweep him off his feet.

Patsie had the liberty of having time off one weekend in May 1944, and headed to the Crescent Ball Room in Tacoma, Washington. Coincidentally, his future wife would be there, too, having arrived in Tacoma earlier that day on a train from Wyoming.

Dolores Jean Hume, 16, who had been a popular high school drum major, went to the dance with her cousin Lois, 17, a tall, slender blonde. Dolores, on a whim to sound French, earlier adopted the name of "Jeneé" as her best friend Bernita adopted the name "Berneé."

Jeneé told the story in a 2000 recorded interview with her son Scotti:

Jeneé and Patsie enjoying some time together while he was in the Navy.

Jeneé in her drum major uniform.

> 'Dolores, you want to go dancing? There's dancing every night from 8 to 12 down at the Crescent Ball Room,' Lois said.
>
> So, we got dressed and went to the Crescent Ball Room, where we danced with a bunch of different people. There were hundreds of servicemen there, but I never liked anybody but sailors. I loved sailors.
>
> We stood there, and quickly, from the other side of the room came this handsome, curly-haired, green-eyed sailor.
>
> I said to Lois, 'Oh, my God, look at that thing coming across the floor.'
>
> 'I was looking at him,' she said to me with the emphasis on "I"—and I said, 'Yeah, you'll probably get him, too, but he's coming this way.'

continued on page 22

21

continued from page 21

Lois was so cute and I was kind of fat—I weighed 125 pounds when I met him. But he said to me, 'Would you like to dance?' I nearly jumped into his hand and said, 'Well, sure!' I thought he was the best-looking guy in the whole room. Never in a million years did I think he was coming to see me.

Our eyes just locked on each other's. Then we danced to 'Long Ago (and Far Away)' [a popular song from the 1944 film 'Cover Girl,' recorded by Frank Sinatra and others]:

> Long ago and far away, I dreamed a dream one day,
> And now that dream is here beside me...
> Chills run up and down my spine,
> Aladdin's lamp is mine.
> The dream was not denied me,
> Just one look and then I knew
> That all I longed for long ago was you.

We danced cheek-to-cheek all that night. He was a great dancer and kisser—we kissed on first date! He walked me home, I ran in to tell my mom about him and said, 'I'm going to marry him.'

Well, we went out every night until he shipped out in August.

Joseph L. McGuigan of the Todd Ship Yards turned the ship over to Captain Gordon A. McLean of the Hamlin, with a speech from each. Then the chaplain blessed the ship with a prayer.

The hectic days that followed were not forgotten. I had no idea what a shakedown cruise would be like. I was bewildered by the process as we went up and down Puget Sound within a limited area. Next came the loading of ammunition and supplies. Then we sailed down the coast, rough at the start, calmer as we advanced, but very rough as when we approached the harbor of San Francisco. Finally, we experienced the thrill of steaming under the Golden Gate Bridge. A week of loading more supplies kept us in the busy harbor. After sailing to San Pedro, we tied up alongside an old tanker that was moored to the dock.

U.S.S. Hamlin, AV-15, was to care for seaplanes whose work was reconnaissance and rescue. We sailed from San Pedro to Hawaii, Eniwetok, Saipan, Tinian, Guam, Ulithi, Iwo Jima, Kerama Retto, Okinawa and finally into Tokyo Bay for the occupation of Japan and the signing of the peace treaty—an 18-month cruise.

As Patsie's Navy experiences grew, he saw an opportunity to combine his interests in shipbuilding and welding into something new and challenging—deep sea diving. He underwent four weeks of second class diver training at the U.S. Naval Net Depot in Tiburon, California, near San Francisco.

Patsie quickly learned he was very good at it. As a result, he became one of the top go-to people for salvage and repair duties. This was fortuitous because divers received bonus pay of an extra $5 per hour for the work—a fact that Patsie underlined in his training manual. Little did he know that he would tally a total of 1,200 hours diving during his 26 months with the Navy. And once more, while others toiled away in the armed forces during the war, against all odds Patsie spent his time improving his skill set and making additional money.

And, while Patsie's training didn't soft-pedal the occupational dangers that came with deep sea diving, neither did he fear the hazards that scared others away. The most dreaded mishap was to fall rapidly for a lengthy amount of time while diving. Pressure would increase on every square inch of the diver, forcing his body into the rigid helmet, which would result in death.

"Blowing up" (becoming too buoyant and ascending too fast) was the second most feared accident. This is why divers were taught to ascend slowly when coming up to surface, allowing their bodies time to adjust to changes in water pressure. This was accomplished by stopping and resting at certain depths. If a diver came to the surface too quickly, he could develop "The Bends," or decompression sickness, which could be fatal if not treated promptly.

Patsie aboard the U.S.S. Hamlin, second one in at right, middle row.

Another danger was the development of an air embolism. This tended to happen when a diver voluntarily or involuntarily held his breath while ascending. Patsie's training manual warned that men have been killed coming from a depth of as little as 10 or 15 feet.

As part of his training, Patsie also studied the precautions of recovering a torpedo from the bottom of the sea floor and dealing with dynamite—both extremely high-risk situations. And, in addition to fully understanding the dangers of diving, communication signals (such as tugging on the lifeline) had to be mastered. Patsie learned that four tugs meant, "Haul me up," while a series of two quick pulls three times in a row meant, "I am all fouled up and need the help of another diver."

He also discovered a diver could communicate with the surface through a telephone hookup—although because of the limited technological advancements of the time, the diver had to stop his air flow to hear the conversations and this communication was minimally used. But if all else failed, there was always the old standby of a slate and pencil lowered from the surface by a line.

CHAPTER 2

Patsie and his diving buddy, who maintained his life line on the surface.

Patsie's diving manual that he used aboard the Hamlin.

To graduate from diving school, a diver had to be able to remain at depths of up to 30 feet for at least one hour, up to 60 feet for at least 30 minutes, and up to 90 feet for at least 20 minutes. Divers could make only one significant dive per day. Any more than that could take a serious toll on their bodies.

PATSIE GETS IN GOOD WITH THE CAPTAIN

Once, while the U.S.S. *Hamlin* had been sailing for only a few hours and was still in Puget Sound, the anchor chain became tangled in the ship's propeller.

Captain Gordon A. McLean called for the best diver on board.

Patsie donned his deep-sea diving suit, dropped into the deep, and untangled the chain. By doing so, Patsie made a name for himself as a "can-do" problem-solver. From then on, any time the captain needed a solution, he'd call upon Patsie because he thought the young sailor could meet any challenge.

25

Patsie was taught how to use an underwater torch to cut and weld, how to fit pipes, patch holes, and work with dynamite (difficult tasks above the surface, much less 30 feet below). He also learned to keep his diver's knife handy for emergencies; for instance, he might need to cut off his weighted boots to ascend to the surface. Every one of these became new skills Patsie relied upon during his time in the Navy.

There was something else that became obvious during Patsie's service: While it may be common to think of the Navy as having mostly battleships and aircraft carriers, the U.S.S. *Hamlin* was more of a support craft than anything—it carried seaplanes and housed 113 officers and 964 enlisted men who were skilled in everything imaginable: from building a seadrome floating air strip at Iwo Jima to recovering downed aircraft at Kerama Retto, just west of Okinawa.

As a result, these men could do it all. And, Patsie joined an elite team— the brave and courageous men who, like him, were willing to risk their lives for their country.

In Hawaii, island girls were more than willing to pose with U.S. sailors.

When the *Hamlin* first reached its first destination, Hawaii, it took on supplies. The next stop was Eniwetok Atoll in the Marshall Islands, some

CHAPTER 2

2,000 miles away. Not long after this stop, the ship participated in several South Pacific campaign battles, including those at Iwo Jima and Okinawa.

Once again, Patsie found himself on the right side of luck and survived—unlike more than 18,000 of his countrymen, who died during the two battles. After they were over, Patsie was called upon for diving work. For example, when a ship was torpedoed, or there was a problem under the waterline, he would help build coffer dams to separate the water from the damaged area. Then, he would cover the holes with metal plates, weld them together to seal the holes, and prepare the site so crews could pump water out the ship. Once "dried," the ship could be towed to floating dry docks.

During combat, Patsie was often part of a boat crew that picked up fliers who were floating in the sea and awaiting rescue after bailing out of crashing planes.

It was not always successful. The crew's orders were to only make one attempt to pick up a flier, who would attempt to grab a rope ring as the boat sped by. Some were unable to accomplish that, and Patsie took it hard as he witnessed it. But he found the strength to carry on, knowing that the next airman would be depending on him.

The *Hamlin*'s first real view of bloody warfare occurred at Iwo Jima. The ship arrived on February 21, 1945—just two days after the battle had begun. Quickly, victims of the intense fight began to pour aboard the ship.

The next day, when the American flag was raised on Mt. Suribachi, everyone who was present and able went on deck to observe the Stars and Stripes. This historic flag-raising was captured in a famous photograph by AP photographer Joe Rosenthal.

During the battle, the *Hamlin* was struck by a four-inch shell, which lodged into its stack. Four men were wounded, but, luckily, the shell did not explode. Three days later, upon routine inspection, the shell was found to be an errant American one—the product of "friendly fire." The shell was carefully heaved overboard, but the incident gave rise to an erroneous report that the *Hamlin* had been hit and sunk.

After the war, Patsie seldom talked about his time in battle, but what he did discuss revealed he had experienced a number of nerve-wracking incidents. Every dive had its dangers. Patsie and his "dive buddy," who monitored his air hoses from the diving boat, developed a camaraderie built on a shared purpose: to look danger in the eye and make danger blink.

These memories of harrowing experiences affected Patsie long after the war ended. Once he returned home, Patsie never again went into the water.

There were other hazards that accompanied the war in the South Pacific: Kamikaze suicide planes and booby-trapped boats were always present during the battles near Japan. Luckily, the *Hamlin* was not struck by suicide planes.

Chaplain Ray recorded that during the three months the *Hamlin* was in port at Kerama Retto, 760 soldiers were buried on Zamami Island, most of them killed by kamikaze attacks.

Once, Patsie and some other crew members were involved in a mission to land on an island to scout it out. After they landed, a typhoon materialized out of nowhere, and the *Hamlin* had to strand the group for several days before returning to rescue them. This was yet another challenging time for Patsie and his shipmates as they feared they had been abandoned.

When the war finally ended on September 2, 1945, the *Hamlin* was anchored just outside Tokyo Bay while the surrender was being signed on the U.S.S. Missouri.

During the war, the *Hamlin* crew was fortunate. Of the nearly 1,110 on board, only 12 were killed; including nine in a tragic seaplane takeoff. Despite being an incredibly stressful situation, Patsie's time aboard the U.S.S. *Hamlin*—and in the Navy—would help shape the man he was quickly becoming.

Here is a timeline of the *Hamlin*'s service:

1944   Jan. 11   Launched
1944   Jun. 26   Commissioned

CHAPTER 2

Patsie poses with his cousin Raymond and Baldo during their time in the Armed Forces.

1944	Aug. 16	Shakedown ended
1944	Aug. 24	Pearl Harbor
1944	Aug. 29	Eniwetok
1944	Sept. 11	Saipan (started tending duty)
1944	Oct. 11	Ulithi
1944	Dec. 29	Saipan
1945	Feb. 15	Guam
1945	Feb. 21	Iwo Jima
1945	Mar. 8	Saipan and Guam
1945	Mar. 23	Departed Saipan
1945	Mar. 28	Kerama Retto
1945	July 11	Chimu Wan, Okinawa
1945	Aug. 16	Departed for Tokyo from Okinawa
1945	Aug. 23	Met destroyer escort U.S.S. Bangust
1945	Sept. 2	Arrived in Tokyo Bay for Japanese surrender
1945	Dec. 15	End Tokyo Bay occupation
1945	Dec. 30	*Hamlin* arrived in Seattle
1947	Jan. 15	Decommissioned
1963	Jan. 1	Struck from Navy List
1972	Nov. 7	Sold for scrap for $87,500

AGAINST ALL ODDS / THE PATSIE CAMPANA STORY

Capt. McLean's message in the U.S.S. Hamlin cruise book.

THE CAPTAIN RECOGNIZES A JOB WELL DONE BY THE CREW

A congratulatory note from Captain Gordon A. McLean to the crew of the U.S.S *Hamlin* underscores his commitment to the men on board. The following is displayed on the opening page of the *Hamlin*'s official cruise book:

> September 26, 1945
> From: The commanding officer
> To: Officers and men of the U.S.S. *Hamlin*
> Subject: Excellent performance of duty
>
> 1. The ending of the war, with the same dramatic suddenness of its beginning, has afforded the first breathing spell that we have had on the ship since our commissioning, just 15 months ago today. While anchored here in Tokyo Bay, finally free from the threat of the crazy kamikaze, we have been individually taking stock of a radically changed situation, and withal there pervades a deep feeling of thankfulness for a sure and timely return to our homes and loved ones.

CHAPTER 2

The *Hamlin* received three bronze stars for the following Asiatic-Pacific Campaigns:
1. Iwo Jima operation: Assault and occupation of Iwo Jima, February 19 to March 8, 1945.
2. Okinawa Gunto operation: Assault and occupation of Okinawa Gunto, March 26 to June 30, 1945.
3. Third Fleet operations against Japan: July 10-25, 1945.

2. I was also thinking of the war cruise of the Hamlin, from Tacoma to Tokyo in 15 months of willing and coordinated effort on the part of this crew which has brought us through the toughest of assignments with flying colors.

The Hamlin proved at Iwo Jima that an air base can be established and operated on a moment's notice in practically any semi-sheltered water on the earth's surface. At Kerama Rhetto in "the most daring seaplane base operation in history" to quote from the Associated Press, we proved that a seaplane base could be established in enemy territory in support of an amphibious operation even before the arrival of the main assault force. The uninterrupted and highly efficient operations carried out by this ship throughout the long suicide siege at Wiseman's Cove was in keeping with the highest traditions of the Naval Service and proved the stamina and unflinching gallantry of you men.

3. In later years you will look back on this cruise with a variety of recollections. Few will recall the days of ease and comfort, some may remember only the long periods of nervous strain and hard work. Most of us, I am sure, will remember an epic story of a group of greenhorns who was the spirit and "stuff" so characteristic of Americans, became an unbeatable Navy crew in a period of three months. The war cruise of the Hamlin represents a very worthwhile period in your lives. You may well be proud of it as am I of you.

Captain Gordon Alexander McLean
Commanding Officer

CHAPTER 3

HOME FROM THE WAR... AS LOVE BLOSSOMS

It had been a fateful evening in 1944 when Navy shipfitter Patsie Campana met Jeneé Hume. They were love-struck at first sight. Starting with a distant glance, a few seconds later they were dancing cheek-to-cheek. Unbeknownst to either, this would be the birth of a romance. It culminated in a June 8, 1946, wedding, in Powell, Wyoming, and then led to 47 years of married life together.

When Patsie shipped out in August 1944, the two had a tearful parting. They pledged their love to each other, but each also knew there was a possibility Patsie might never return—the odds were stacked against him.

"You go ahead and date," Patsie told her. "I don't know if I'll be back."

But Jeneé had faith. She told the guys she met that she had a boyfriend—and he was overseas. She kept Patsie's photo by the radio at home, and patiently waited for his return.

On December 30, 1945, after World War II had ended, the U.S.S. *Hamlin* finally arrived back in Tacoma. Its captain had prepared a special treat for one of his most valued shipmen.

"Where does your girlfriend live?" the captain asked, remembering the good-looking girl whose picture he'd seen in Patsie's quarters.

"In Tacoma." Patsie replied.

"Well," the captain said, "I'm going to let the gangplank down, and I'm going to let you be the first off because you deserve it. Then, it's going back up."

And that's exactly what the captain did.

The entire crew watched Patsie get off the ship. Many could hardly contain themselves. They were a bit angry and envious. But none complained out of respect for a job well done by Patsie during the most challenging of times.

Now on the mainland, Patsie headed straight to Tacoma to see Jeneé, glowing with anticipation.

He arrived still wearing his blue dress sailor uniform.

Jeneé, in her white chenille robe, opened the door. Surprised, she hugged him tightly and shed chenille yarn bits all over his uniform.

The two laughed while meticulously picking off each piece of lint.

Jeneé was thrilled to have her Patsie home, but there was a slight problem: she had accepted a date with an insistent sailor from Chicago who, like Patsie, came from an Italian family. And he was on his way over to pick her up.

With Patsie's surprise arrival, Jeneé did not have enough time to try to reach the sailor and therefore was unable to get in touch with him to cancel their date.

When the suitor arrived to pick up Jeneé, Patsie was in her home. The doorbell rang and Jeneé answered it. She knew who it was.

The sailor stood there with a smile on his face as Jeneé stood in the doorway and told him he had to leave.

The sailor, confused, refused.

But Jeneé went back inside as quickly as she could, knowing Patsie would be furious about the new man.

Sure enough, Patsie flew through the door and told the Chicagoan, "You better get the hell out of here!"

In an instant, Patsie knocked him off the porch.

The man rolled down the house's 19 steps to the sidewalk along South Ash Street, never to return.

With that matter settled, Patsie got right to the point: He asked Jeneé for her hand in marriage.

Jeneé giddily said, "Hey, yeah! Why don't we try that?"

The couple set right to work in planning their next move, but this too had its own complications—something they would conquer together. Even though the war had ended, Patsie was still an active service member. He would not complete his military obligations until April 2, 1946. But, Patsie had secured a 13-day leave from the *Hamlin*'s captain so that he and Jeneé could visit Lorain, meet his folks, and pick out a ring. And this became yet another adventure for the couple.

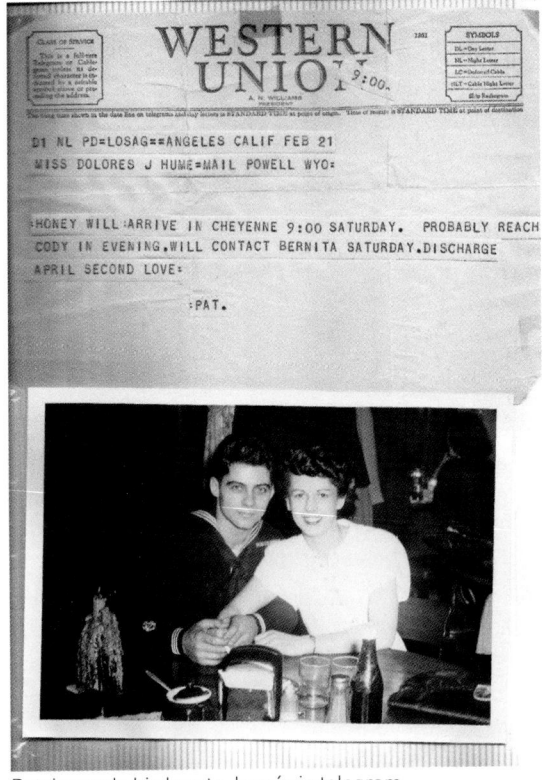

Patsie sends his love to Jeneé via telegram as the wedding nears.

AGAINST ALL ODDS / THE PATSIE CAMPANA STORY

The Humes lived in an adobe home in Wyoming that they built by hand.

TEENAGER JENEÉ VISITS LORAIN AND HAS "THE WORST 13 DAYS OF HER LIFE"

When 18-year-old Jeneé learned that Patsie had a 13-day leave as his ship came home, they planned a trip to Lorain, Ohio, to meet the Campana family.

The experience wasn't what she expected.

After getting permission from her parents and telling them she was going to get engaged, Jeneé boarded a train with Patsie (in separate sleepers, of course) and headed for Lorain—and culture shock.

Being from a poor homesteader family in Wyoming, and having once lived in an adobe home, Jeneé wasn't prepared for the reality of a traditional Italian-Catholic family.

First, before she got off the train, Patsie asked a favor of her: "I don't want you smoking around my folks; they hate it. My dad thinks it makes a woman look like a whore."

Jeneé agreed not to smoke.

Additionally, Jeneé was used to hugs and kisses when loved ones reunited, but there wasn't much emotion among the Campana's upon

CHAPTER 3

Patsie's return. The first time she met Maria Campana, she was a little cool, speaking only in Italian.

"I think she didn't like me, because I wasn't Italian and I wasn't Catholic," she said. "I wasn't from Lorain, Ohio. Patsie could've married the girl next door or across the street. Aunt Rosemary [Patsie's sister] thought it was terrible for me to even talk like that, but it was the truth."

Jeneé thought her future father-in-law, Thomas Campana, was a sweetheart and called Albert and Rosemary (Patsie's siblings) "cute." She also met many other relatives and got a real taste of an Italian extended family. That included Rose DeTillio, godmother to the Campana children, who would go on to become Jeneé's good friend. Other names that became family were Tommy Scappucci, Tina, Dennis, and Aggie.

"We were on leave for 13 days—the worst 13 days of my life. I felt like such an outsider. Nobody embraced me. They just said, 'Hello.' Patsie arrived home, and his mother had the most wonderful feast on the table—breaded veal, homemade soup, everything. Pa probably got somebody around the corner to tend the bar while he ate, and there I was with all those Italians—and Ma said to Patsie, 'You better go in and take care of the bar while Pa sleeps, OK?'"

"Can you imagine? He just got home from the war."

But as time went on, Jeneé became a favorite of Maria Campana. Jeneé's personality, humility, and frugality scored points with Maria, as did her total, loving support of Patsie.

Back to Tacoma

After the chaos of visiting friends and relatives, buying a ring, and formally proposing on his knee ("He was romantic from the beginning," Jeneé recalled), the couple hopped back on a train to Tacoma so Patsie could return to the ship and active duty.

When he reported to the *Hamlin*, Patsie was pleasantly surprised when the captain insisted he now take a 31-day leave, denying he had ever given him an earlier 13-day leave.

Patsie didn't argue. He and Jeneé then headed to her parents' house in Tacoma.

Jeneé asked Patsie, "Well, are you going to go back to Lorain?"

"No," he replied. "If you've got a bed around here and your folks will let me stay, I will stay here with you guys."

Jeneé's mother, Edna, was tickled. She said, "You know you can stay."

The two had a great time during that month. The Hume family, Dave, Edna, Dick and baby brother Bobby, grew fond of Patsie. Patsie and Dick would even have cooking contests to pass the time—whose cake was better, the chocolate or the white?

A page from Patsie and Jeneé's scrapbook celebrating their engagement.

CHAPTER 3

When Patsie's 31-day leave ended, he once again reported to the captain for duty.

"When are you going to take a leave?" the captain asked him.

"Well, I had 13 days and I had 31," Patsie replied.

With yet another contrary answer, the captain said, "Oh, you didn't have nothing. Here's a leave for 30 days with pay."

The Hume family: Dick, Edna, Jeneé, David and Bobby.

Again, Patsie followed orders and decided to head back to Tacoma to stay with the Humes. During this leave, he helped the family move back to Wyoming.

In Wyoming, Patsie made himself useful to the Humes. He helped around the house, fixing what was broken and putting in improvements such as a new floor and new washer and dryer. He became close friends with Dick Hume, Jeneé's brother. *[The friendship between Dick and Patsie continued throughout their lives. Patsie later brought Dick to Lorain to live near them and gave him a job. As Dick aged and had difficulty walking, Patsie bought him a golf cart to get around on the sprawling company grounds.]*

PATSIE TRIES HIS HAND AT BEING A COWBOY

When they returned to Powell, Wyoming, after leaving Tacoma, the Hume family moved back into their farmhouse. During that time, Jeneé's father, David, left his horses out wild.

"Why don't you go round up those horses, Patsie?" he asked of his future son-in-law.

David was more and more impressed every day with Patsie's ability to do most anything, even learning to ride decked out in cowboy chaps.

"All right," he said, "I think I'll use your truck."

"Go ahead; do what you want to do," David replied as he went on to sit in a corner chair and laugh his butt off.

Patsie tests out his horseback riding skills while staying with the Humes.

Patsie got some barley and some five-gallon pails and put them in the back of the truck. He set the pails in the middle of the field. The food attracted the horse and some came up to eat the barley. Patsie couldn't lasso them all, but he did get one. However, the stubborn creature wouldn't move.

Undeterred, Patsie tied the rope to the truck's bumper and started to pull the horse back to the corral, dragging him at times. The thought going through Patsie's mind was, "That SOB; he is going to come back one way or the other."

After Patsie returned, David Hume rounded up the remaining horses.

A Wyoming wedding and adventurous honeymoon

When April 1945 rolled around, Patsie, now 26 years old, was finally discharged from active military service. The couple soon made final plans for a June 8 wedding in Powell, Wyoming.

As the wedding date neared, there were things Patsie and Jeneé still had to work out: She became Catholic so the ceremony could be held at St. Barbara's Church in Powell, Wyoming. Patsie told Jeneé she didn't have to change her religious affiliation, but he wasn't changing his. However, Jeneé treasured the vision of her husband and family all going to Mass every Sunday, so she joined the Catholic Church.

Patsie and Jeneé with their wedding party, June 8, 1946.

"We had a very nice wedding, but we didn't have much money," Jeneé recalled in a 2001 interview. "I could've had money for a wedding, but I spent what I had on clothes."

Meanwhile, Patsie was still waiting for his mustering-out pay of $100 and diving bonus of more than $6,000.

Baldo Campana served as the best man. Jeneé's uncles, Ralph and Glenn Harris, were ushers. Uncle Glenn's daughter was the flower girl, and Bernita Rogers was the maid of honor.

Georgia Galvin and Ruth Eastman were bridesmaids. Georgia was a good friend of Jeneé's, and Ruth was Uncle Dick's fiancée. Unfortunately, Dick and Ruth didn't last long as a couple. He joined the Army in May 1946, and they married the following July, but Ruth soon wanted out and wrote him a Dear John letter when he was serving overseas.

AGAINST ALL ODDS / THE PATSIE CAMPANA STORY

Patsie and Jeneé on their wedding day.

Maria Campana came to the wedding with Patsie's baby sister Rosemary. Maria had a different idea of a proper wedding, and because of this, she was kind of demanding. For example, she disagreed with the menu—they were serving sandwiches instead of having Italian wedding soup.

Jeneé's mother, Edna, wasn't the best cook—especially when compared to Maria. So, Maria brought her own salami, bread, cheese, and knife.

About half an hour after the wedding, Patsie decided his mother had made enough trouble. He put her in Uncle Dick's car, drove her to the bus station, and told her to go home. She had no choice but to head back to Lorain.

The newlyweds then set out on a seven-week honeymoon, flush with some $6,000-plus from Patsie's bonus pay. They borrowed Uncle Dick's Model A Ford convertible with a leaky roof and headed out on the scenic Beartooth Highway through Yellowstone National Park and into Red Lodge and Billings, Montana.

CHAPTER 3

At Yellowstone, Patsie tried to feed a baby grizzly bear and barely got back into the car in time to escape an enraged mother who chased him. From there, it rained all the way to Billings, where they decided to look up the luxurious Northern Hotel. Since the convertible leaked so badly, Patsie and Jeneé were both soaked and quite worn out from the drive.

"Patsie had to drive; he had one foot on the gas pedal and one on the clutch, and I had my feet up in the air, but I was getting wet. We didn't care about going into the hotel all wet and disheveled, but they said no, they didn't have any rooms," Jeneé remembered how their appearance may have played a factor.

Their sightseeing continued into the Midwest and ended in Lorain, Ohio. The couple spent nearly all their money, but they had the time of their lives.

Back to Lorain

When Patsie and Jeneé decided to stay in Lorain full-time, they initially lived with Thomas and Maria Campana at 1850 Washington Avenue for about a year while Thomas finished building the apartments upstairs.

Since Patsie was busy working at the National Tube Co. during the day and tending bar at night, Jeneé was left with her in-laws—and her new best friend, Rose DeTillio. The two had hit it off when Jeneé had first visited Lorain and Rose encouraged Jeneé to call her when she moved to town.

"Thank God for Rose. Otherwise I probably would've left Pat!" Jeneé once said.

Patsie and Jeneé with their wedding cake.

Maria, Patsie, Jeneé, Baldo and Rosemary.

Rose became a dear family friend as well as a mother figure for Jeneé, teaching her to be a homemaker. Patsie and Jeneé honored both Rose and her husband Mike by asking them to be godparents to all six children. When they were "on the road" with the family over the years, Rose and Mike would always travel to help out when a new little Campana was born, when Jeneé's mother was no longer able to do so. Patsie always had a deep respect for Rose DeTillio; they understood each other and they were dear friends. He appreciated how loving and supporting she and her family were to his family.

When the apartments were finished, Patsie and Jeneé moved into their new quarters. Shortly afterward, their first child, David, was born in 1948. A daughter they named Patti arrived in 1949. Another son, Larry, was born in 1954. Pat Jr. ("Corky") came in 1957, Bobby in 1959, and Scotti in 1968.

Over those years, Patsie would move his family across five states—all in the heart of steel mill country. Despite the chaos, he was determined to keep everyone together. As a result, any long-distance arrangements were out of the question.

Finally, their last stop was back where it all began: Lorain. And this

CHAPTER 3

time, everything came together—the experience and confidence Patsie had gained, the wonderful family that had grown to six children, and the desire to put down roots. That led to Patsie once again succeeding against all odds and building a long-lasting legacy. But before any of that happened, Patsie had to discover how to put his calling to work.

Patsie with co-workers in Italy.

PART TWO

BUILDING A FAMILY AND BECOMING A BUSINESSMAN

CHAPTER 4

FINDING A NICHE IN THE BUSINESS WORLD

With World War II over, America saw an economic boom that would last for decades. Patsie Campana, a man of many talents, had a world of employment opportunities at his doorstep. He just had to decide what it was he really wanted to do.

As fate would have it, his family's Campana Café was the first concern. As the oldest son, Patsie's father, Thomas, wanted him to operate the business—and he couldn't easily refuse. It worked out well, because as a newlywed, Patsie knew he had to support Jeneé and build a nest egg, so he tended bar in the evening while working days for National Tube Co. But as the tavern demanded more and more of Patsie's time, he began to realize this was not the life he wanted for himself. He had higher ambitions…. even if he hadn't yet figured out how to put his skill set to more productive use.

Since Patsie had returned to Lorain, he reacquainted himself with old friends and new connections. He also made next ones. This led to Patsie landing a full-time job as an electrician for the R.T. Patterson Co., a leading electrical construction company that was starting to make a name for itself in Cleveland. He also became a journeyman in the International Brotherhood of Electrical Workers Local 129. While his father wanted Patsie to work alongside him, he recognized his son was meant for bigger things.

AGAINST ALL ODDS / THE PATSIE CAMPANA STORY

CAMPANA CAFÉ WAS A NEIGHBORHOOD WATERING HOLE INTO THE 1990S

The Campana Café in later years.

The Campana Café became a tavern when the Prohibition era ended in 1933. Thomas Campana had built a neighborhood market in 1926, later adding a café. When his father offered Patsie the chance to manage the bar after World War II, he quit his job and ran the Campana Café for about six weeks.

It didn't work out.

Thomas wouldn't relinquish control of the money, and Patsie felt his hands were being tied. After his experience earning substantial money in the shipyard, and knowing what his Navy deep sea diving had earned him, Patsie felt there were more lucrative ways to use his talents.

As it turned out, Thomas actually wanted to have his younger son, Albert, run the bar. But Thomas felt obligated to go through the formal, Italian, oldest-son-gets-the-option tradition, and so Patsie gave it a try. Thomas also quickly realized it wasn't for his oldest son.

While Thomas continued to own the bar until 1962, his son Albert and Albert's wife, Alberta, managed it for years after. Patsie's sister, Rosemary Hribar, and her husband Pete, also ran it for a few years before it became a social club. In the mid-1990s, it was converted into an office building, and remains so today.

Patsie's oldest son, David, was the tavern's manager after his college graduation in 1971 for a time. Even 40 years after it opened, it was still a small, neighborhood bar that catered to an ethnic crowd of Italians, Poles, and Russians.

At that time, a small glass of beer was 20 cents, and a fishbowl was 30 cents. A bottle of Stroh's beer was 30 cents, and a bottle of a premium beer was 45 cents. A shot of bar whiskey had to be a generous ounce—the customers were frugal, blue-collar types who wanted the most for their money. The bottom shelf whiskey—Seagram's, Old Log Cabin, and Old Thompson—was 40 cents a shot. The middle shelf liquors, such as Bacardi rum, were 45 cents. Finally, the top shelf, which included Cutty Sark scotch and Maker's Mark bourbon, were 50 cents a shot. Hamburgers were 35 cents each.

At the end of the day in 1971-72, if sales hit $200, it was a big day.

CHAPTER 4

Over the next few years, Patsie advanced at Patterson—first to project manager, then field manager, and then general manager of Patterson's Cleveland division. This was the beginning of the journey that Patsie and his growing family would travel for the next two decades.

When Patsie joined R.T. Patterson Co., he was the company's sixth Cleveland employee. Among Patterson's prestigious roster of clients were steel industry stalwarts Bethlehem Steel and U.S. Steel. In 1950, as one of his first major assignments, Patsie worked with general manager Dave Patterson on a project for Bethlehem Steel in Johnstown, Pennsylvania.

Then, over the next three years, Patsie and Dave worked 12-hour days for a major U.S. Steel project in Fairless Hills, Pennsylvania. Patterson helped build a hot strip mill and slab mill on that site, which became the largest steel works ever built at the time. (Unfortunately, in 1992, most of that steel mill closed.)

The project site was across the Delaware River from Trenton, New Jersey, in what was once a cow pasture. The property was fenced in, and when dinner time came around, Jeneé prepared dinner for Patsie, took David and Patti to the site so they could see their father, and passed his dinner over the fence so he would have something to eat.

Patsie said this about the massive project: "It's where a million man-hours were welded together in two or three years by a crew of 500 to 600 men in a mill over a third of a mile long and 500 feet wide."

After the assignment, Patsie barely had time to catch his breath before the company sent him to tackle a new one. He didn't mind. But he longed for Jeneé and the children constantly while they were apart as their togetherness was very important. So, if that meant bringing the family along to stay in temporary lodging, Patsie did so. As a result, his job with Patterson meant a lot of moving and travel.

There were 18 moves, some of which included more than one move per location. From their home in Lorain, where David and Patti were born, in 1950, the family moved to Johnstown, Pennsylvania. Then, they moved to Philadelphia, where in 1954 their son Larry was born.

A Trenton, New Jersey, move followed. And then off to Detroit and Dearborn, Michigan, and then Weirton, West Virginia, where Pat and Bobby were born.

A scrapbook page of Patsie and Jeneé having fun.

Of all the locations, only in one—Dearborn—did the family own a home. There, Patsie spent time and effort fixing it up, only to sell it in a few months without making a profit. The rest of the homes the family lived in were rentals.

Finding a house with enough bedrooms and space for Patsie's growing family was a challenge. The Campanas secured one rental house in Weirton that was on the side of a sizeable hill. The view out the back window of the bedrooms was just the hill's sheer drop.

While Patsie was busy at work, Jeneé had her hands full with David, Patti, and Larry, especially while expecting Pat Jr., because Larry had a lot of energy and enjoyed running around. Because the house in

CHAPTER 4

Weirton was on such a steep hillside, Jeneé put a harness on him (in those days, such harnesses were available and families thought they were OK for occasional use). So, Larry wore a harness hooked to a clothesline, enabling him to run the full length of the line, but not fall over the edge of the hill.

Once, Jeneé's father, David Hume, visited. He saw what his daughter had done with her son and was unhappy with the harness on Larry. Even though he was a calm, laid-back man, he let Jeneé know it was disgusting to tie Larry to the clothesline like a dog. But, Jeneé explained, she had to do what she had to do to keep her family safe.

The Campanas remained in Weirton for about four years, which gave them a chance to settle down. Jeneé took up bowling, and became active in PTA. Patsie, likewise, became quite a bowler in his free time. Two clippings from The Weirton Daily Times list him on the Patterson-Emerson-Comstock team, rolling a series of 381 in October 1957 and 469 in December 1957.

In 1959, immediately after Bobby was born, the company sent Patsie overseas, to Cornigliano, Italy, to finish a job started by a foreman who had died. Patsie spent nearly two months in Europe, finishing off the trip with visits to Barrea, Paris, Normandy and Lourdes (the pilgrimage site where the Virgin Mary is reported to have appeared).

The original plan was to move the entire family to Italy for two years once Bobby was old enough to travel.

The Italian visit was a long and stressful separation for Patsie and his family. Now the mother of five children, Jeneé insisted the family head back temporarily to Lorain, where there was support from a wide circle of relatives and friends while Patsie was gone.

"While Patsie was in Italy, I drove five kids back to Lorain from Weirton, West Virginia, by myself. And I told him that he either comes home or I'm going back to Wyoming. That's when I nearly had a breakdown," Jeneé said in an interview in 2000. And though she didn't realize it at the time, this was a move back to Lorain for good.

Patsie with R.T and Dave Patterson.

Patsie continued with Patterson for another eight years before taking his talents to the Hatfield Electric Co. His work with the Pattersons helped him come into his own. One story claims that the Pattersons saw Patsie as a diamond in the rough.

Dave Patterson, one of the owners, once said, "Look, Patsie, we gave you a chance, made you a field engineer, then superintendent, but you are still Moses in the high grass. You've got to beat that grass down…"

The point was that once a person beats down the grass blocking him from excelling, he'll unleash his hidden talent and reach new heights. For Patsie, it was a lesson that required an experience rather than simply words.

So, one day, R.T. Patterson approached Patsie and asked, "Are you busy?"

Patsie answered, "I'm busier than hell."

R.T. nodded, and asked Patsie to go with him to the nearby racetrack at Waterford Downs (now the Mountaineer Casino, Racetrack and Resort).

Extremely overwhelmed with work, Patsie declined.

But Patterson wouldn't stand for that. "Oh, is your job so screwed up you can't leave it?" he countered.

Patsie gave the matter some thought, and replied, "Wait a bit. And, I'm not going for one day; I'm going for three."

Off the two men went. They enjoyed themselves at the races.

Two weeks later, Dave Patterson stopped to check in on Patsie and found him looking newly alive.

"Patsie," he told him, "I think you've beat the grass down."

CHAPTER 4

It was a compliment that made the entire exchange one of the brightest moments in Patsie's life. He had earned validation from a respected leader, and recognized he now not only had the skill and experience he needed, but also the confidence to achieve any goal he desired.

By 1966, Patsie decided the time had arrived: he would strike out on his own. But it wouldn't be immediately. Instead, he accepted a four-year contract with Hatfield Electric Co., a company with clients such as the Terminal Tower in Cleveland. Patsie was determined to be deliberate, and planned to spend those four years developing the foundation for his own company.

Patsie was with Hatfield Electric for four years.

One example of how Patsie started to think out of the box was when Hatfield needed a location in Lorain. Patsie located some property, built an office for the company, and then leased the building to Hatfield—which was a shrewd business deal. And with Patsie's old connections with customers such as U.S. Steel, he used his network to land electrical jobs for Hatfield, once called the "king" of electrical contractors in the area.

Hatfield would later land big projects like the Justice Center in Cleveland and One Cleveland Center. Unfortunately, the company could not remain competitive during the 1980s recession, and in 1987 declared bankruptcy.

In 1967, Patsie was named vice president of Hatfield Electric and put in charge of the steel mills division. At the same time, the Campana Company was taking shape. Jeneé would be a key player in its formation.

What was the recipe for Patsie Campana's secret sauce? The answer was found in numerous letters he wrote to his family while on the career-defining Patterson project he handled in Italy.

PATSIE DEVELOPS AN ESTIMATION GUIDE, TAKES CORRESPONDENCE COURSES

When a job with Patterson-Emerson-Comstock (as it was later known) or Hatfield Electric was finished, Patsie Campana was not. He evaluated each project, having recorded how long it took to do each task and then figured out how many man-hours it had required. That way, when he submitted a bid for his next job, he knew how long the job would take and what the costs would be.

With this information, Patsie developed a manual he would use when he founded his own company. It became a crucial part of his business, and its accuracy would rival that of today's software programs that industries use to put bids together.

During the 1950s, Patsie also took correspondence courses through the International Correspondence Schools of Scranton, Pa. He studied engineering and math. What he learned assisted him with creating his manual.

CHAPTER 5

HOME AND AWAY: A LETTER WRITER SHARES DEEP THOUGHTS

Even though it wasn't until 1966 when Patsie decided to begin planning to launch his own company, letters he wrote earlier reveal the foundation for those plans, offering insight to his state of mind working for someone else with little control over his fate.

While he was out of town—and sometimes out of the country—on business, Patsie wrote frequent letters to his family. The letters reveal a softer side of the "take-charge" Patsie, and show that as he approached age 40, he was entering his prime and felt he had been blessed in both family and career.

Patsie understood that much of his life to that point had been a result of overcoming the odds against him. He had taken numerous risks that paid off—a hazardous stint in the military, a gutsy decision to remove himself from his father's tavern business, and a brave choice to balance a demanding job with an equally demanding family.

Letters he wrote to Jeneé in 1959, when he worked in Cornigliano, Italy, for the Patterson company offer a glimpse into how much he loved his family amidst having to devote a considerable amount of time to his job.

He wrote of his passion for Jeneé, feelings that were still on fire after 13 years of marriage, and how it pained him to be apart from her.

In the following letter, Patsie shares his feelings on the matter with Jeneé, knowing that the plan was for the Campana family to spend two years in Italy:

> *My Dearest Darling,*
>
> *Here it is in Italy and I am writing you from the job office... Everyone was expecting me, and I got a good reception from the Italians here. I know I will learn to speak good Italian after I am here for a while, or should I say in about four weeks.*
>
> *I have been told by Dave Patterson that they really need someone to stay here bad and that I could probably get what I wanted and more...*
>
> *The conveniences here are up to date except that there are not too many single homes, but a lot of apartments. We could easily get maid service at a decent rate. The school situation here is not what I believed as far as English schooling...*
>
> *I am sure you would get along well here but it will take some time to adjust to the Italians. These people are much nicer than the people next door.*
>
> *I miss you and the children and will count the days till I hold you in my arms again. I love you so terribly much and miss you so. Give my kids a big hug from Daddy.*
>
> *I hope this letter finds you all in good health.*
>
>
>
> *All my love forever.*
> Pat
>
>

At one point, he wrote about bringing the family over to Italy for a couple of months. He wrote:

CHAPTER 5

My Dearest Darling and Darlings,

Today I was in a meeting for the job, and I conducted the entire meeting. The Italians congratulated me afterwards and told me what a good job I have been doing. They said I would be valuable assisting them on the Blooming Mill shutdown… they insisted that I stay on and asked what inducement they could give me to stay. I told them as of now, none. Perhaps if things go well I can bring you all here for three or four months until the job is complete. If not, then I am coming home.

I am so glad you had all the assistance from the Weirton people [the company helped the Campanas with moving from Weirton, W. Va., to Lorain] *and I say "God Bless Them" and shall say a special prayer for them Easter Sunday. Send me the "bill" for moving, and I will send it to P.E.C.* [Patterson-Emerson-Comstock Co.]*.*

Hi David. How do you like Lorain? Will you write your Daddy a letter and tell me about it?

Hi Patti. Do you like your new school and have you played with Carol and the twins?

Hi Larry. Daddy loves you also and misses you so.

Mommy. Mommy, I love you so. The tears come to my eyes when I think of my beautiful family. I went to church last Sunday and will go this Sunday and pray to "God" for your safekeeping.

All my love forever, yours only
Pat

After a bit, Patsie was feeling confident about the job he was doing. However, he struggled with how much he missed his family and worried about them. He wrote:

My Dearest Darling,

Here is 11 a.m. and the job is in full swing.

I have quite a bit to say here [about the operation] *and the workers all listen to me and respect me. They tell me that they noticed how jealous the other fellows* [managers from the P.E.C. company] *are but I told him I didn't think so. But between you and I, we know so.*

Answering some of your questions, Mommy, I don't know where I will work. I'm going to try to get a couple weeks off so you and I can be together. I don't want you to forget about your promise about spending every minute with me all the time I am off.

I don't want you and the children here in the apartment and that is why I am coming home as fast as possible. It's beautiful here but I don't like the idea of living in an apartment not having enough room for the kids to play.

Your mom, bless her; she doesn't realize how much I appreciate her [Edna Hume was helping Jeneé with the children]. *Mac Curley is my boss but he treats me fine…*

Mom, I get $16 per day [for expenses] *and I pay for my own room and meals. My hotel is $4.50 a day and the meals cost about $6 per day. The food is all right but is not the Italian food that we are used to.*

Hold onto the bills for moving and I will send it in when I return.

Oh, Doll, baby, you are all my life. I love you so. It won't be long now and I will return home to you and our beautiful children. I'm so glad that the children are enjoying themselves. That is one of the reasons why I may give up P.E.C. It's about time we all begin to have our roots one place. I don't really promise to settle down I don't exactly promise to settle down but we will try.

CHAPTER 5

The office getting crowded and I'm fielding too many questions so I will close.

All my love forever,
Your loving husband
Pat

In March 1959, the Campana's landlord jacked up the rent for their Weirton, W.Va., house. Jeneé decided she wasn't going to pay that much and moved the family back to Lorain. Patsie felt bad he was not home when the family relocated. He wrote this letter:

Here it is March 24th and slowly but surely the time is going by... I sure feel bad about you moving and me not being there to help. Mom, you're so wonderful! I love you so very much

Mac Curley [of R.T. Patterson Co.] *asked me how long I would stay, and I told him I would stay only as long as this first shutdown. I also told him I would come back if I were needed. I am sure I am...*

Oh, Doll. I love you, I love you, I love you. You're in my mind and my heart at all times. I pray for the time to go by faster so that I can return home to you. I hope you are all settled by the time this letter reaches you. Give the kids a big, big kiss from Daddy. I am glad Bobby is doing so well.

I am wondering what P.E.C. will do with me now that we have moved to Lorain, Ohio. Maybe everything will work out better, and I will settle down to a normal life. Perhaps something good will come of all this. It always has, either way. I don't much care as long as I am with my family. Tell the children that Daddy loves them and will be home soon.

As you know, I am going to Rome and then to France to see Larry. Ask my mother the exact town he is buried in and which cemetery. I am also going to Lourdes in France to pray for my family to the Blessed Virgin Mary.

Your loving husband,
Pat

During his work in Italy, Patsie made it a point to reassure Jeneé of his love for her and their family. He wrote:

My Dearest Darlings,

Today is Friday, and I received another letter from you, and you finally got some of my letters. You now are beginning to realize how much you and the children mean to me. I don't speak too much of the children because I know that when I tell you of my love for you, you will also realize my love for our children. I am sure you will tell them how much their Daddy misses them.

I am glad R.T. called you and volunteered his assistance [with the family's relocation to Lorain]. *It now makes me feel better. I know what my capabilities are and I am sure I am a top man in my field, but I am going to try to consider my family if possible in order to give them a chance for a happier life in Lorain. I am not promising but we will see.*

I love you so very much, and it seems the only way I can express myself is in these few words. I wish I was the eloquent-speaking type that could fit the words together so as to make you understand my true feelings for you.

Tell my folks that Italy is beautiful but I like the U.S.A. much better...

I have about 11 more days to go before I go to Rome. Tell David, Patti, Larry and Corky that Daddy loves them and will be home soon.

CHAPTER 5

All my love forever,
Your loving husband and Daddy,
Pat

Shortly after the previous letter, Patsie followed up with this writing:

My Dearest Darlings,

Hi Mommy! Gosh, but I miss you and the children today. Today [March 29, 1959] is Easter Sunday and this morning we all went to church…

The work is progressing at a good pace and as usual, I have taken over and these Italians recognize me as the top man and all come to me for decisions…

Darling, give me an idea of what I can get you in Italy… I hope you are settled in your new home. I wish I could explain how I feel about you. I think of you and the children constantly. I am going to Rome after the job is over and see my people. Then to Paris and where my brother is [the cemetery where his brother Larry, killed in World War II, is buried] and then right home to you.

I love you so and miss you so. Tell the children than Daddy loves them and thinks of them.

All my love, yours forever,
Pat

In the following letter, Patsie discussed a new opportunity: the steel mill work was nearing completion, but the Italian steel company Cosider S.P.A. asked for Patsie to stay on board. This request came right after Jeneé had given birth to Bobby.

63

My Dearest Darling,

This is now Friday evening 9 p.m. and I just got through having dinner. I had prosciutto and three different kinds of cheese. I do believe I am putting on weight...

I am having the time of my life speaking Italian. They realize that I don't speak the good Italian but they all say that I speak well. I am getting along very well and am very well liked.

We had a P.E.C. meeting and R.T. Patterson told the boys who was to stay and who was to return... The Italian company asked especially for me to stay. I told R.T. that I really don't know what to say for I am always thinking of family and especially after my wife having a baby. So I told him I would give him a decision in two weeks or so. When the two weeks are up, I am going to return to America and stay home until the shutdown of the Blooming Mill, which is supposed to be June 15th.

Also, I could ask them to send for my family and you and the children could be here during vacation time and then you could return around school time and I would come home at the end of September. Let me know what you think of it.

R.T. Patterson watched me operate, and he really is sold on me... he told me what a good man I was and that I would have a job with P.E.C. as long as he lived. The Pattersons really do stick together, don't they?

Darling, I have missed you and the children. I think of you and the children always and I know I could not live without you, I love you so.

I hope the children are well and are helping you with the house work.

CHAPTER 5

Hi David. Are you taking care of things for Daddy?

Hi Patti. How is my big girl?

Hi Larry. Are you being a nice boy?

Daddy misses all you kids so very much. Say hi to Grandma for me [Jeneé's mother Edna Hume is helping with the children].

All my love forever,
Pat

P.S. Let me know what you think I should do about staying till October.

[Editor's note: Jeneé wrote back, "I'm simply a miserable person without you. This is it, Doll. No more of these separations, promise?... When I met with Larry's teacher Larry [then in kindergarten] told me, 'Momma, you'd better tell her I don't have a daddy' real loud, and I said, 'Larry!' And he said, 'Well, I don't anymore. He moved to Italy.' So I told her and she sure laughed. But I don't think Larry believes you are coming back. You've been gone so long. It will be a month in two more days."]

By the end of March, Patsie had firmed up some of his plans about returning to America. He also sounded quite homesick.

Hi Darling,

Today is Tuesday, March 31st, and I received another

of your letters… Darling, you will not have to wait until June to come here. I am coming home very soon. I will be here through April 15th and then I will take a trip to Rome, Barrea, Paris and then home…

Oh Doll baby, I love you. When we are together again, it will be a great day for me… I wish I could let you know what is in my heart. My whole life depends upon you. I pray to God and thank God for the most wonderful wife a man could ever get.

Doll, baby, it is hard to write about this place for I haven't been to many places. I am working every day (but not hard) and haven't seen much of this place. I do know one thing: I'd rather be in the U.S.A. than any other place in the world…

Doll, I will keep writing even if I do repeat myself only to tell you of my love. Give my children my love for me. Thank Mom for all her help and God bless her.

Forever and always,
Your husband,
Pat

Finally, Patsie was ready to wrap up his work in Italy and travel home. In a letter dated April 9, 1959, he describes how he had declined to come back to Italy in June.

My Dearest Most Precious,
It won't be long now till when I get started for Rome and soon home.
Mac Curley asked me if I would like to come back in June, and I told him nothing doing. This is no place for me even if it is Italy. I have a deep feeling for Italy but I have a much deeper feeling for the U.S.A.…

CHAPTER 5

I am so sorry to have you in a small house but when I get back we will know what to do to get settled.

Robert Mark is getting bigger. I probably won't recognize him. Do you think that he will know me? I'll bet Corky [about two years old] *won't know his daddy. Boy, I sure miss you and the children. After I get to Barrea it won't take me long to get home.*

You'd better reserve a couple of days for me to be strictly alone with you!

Your loving husband

PATSIE TENDERLY WRITES TO JENEÉ, OFFERING SUPPORT AS SHE TENDS TO HER ILL MOTHER

In late 1962, Jeneé's mother, Edna Hume, was in failing health. Jeneé went to Wyoming to be by her side. It was kind of a turnabout; just a few years earlier, Edna, despite crippling arthritis, came to Jeneé's side as David, Larry, Patti, and Pat Jr. each were born.

This was a difficult time for Jeneé and the Campana family, who was at the time living back in Lorain. Jeneé was very close to her mother. She had learned how being frugal did not include frugality in how love was shown.

"We were rich with love from both my mom and dad," she once said.

Edna raised chickens, canned fruit and vegetables, and sold milk from the family cows so her children could have a few niceties like the other kids did. Frequently calling each other "Sis" or "Sister," Jeneé was heartbroken when Edna passed away the next year at age 58.

During her absence, Patsie took care of the children with help from relatives. He was deeply affected by his mother-in-law's illness as well,

continued on page 68

continued from page 67

and especially by how Jeneé was handling it. He shared his feelings in a letter to Jeneé, written shortly after she went to Wyoming in late 1962:

> My Dearest,
> It's like old times writing a letter to you reminding me of the Navy days. I really loved you a lot then but it's hard to describe how much more I love you now. When you got on the plane it felt like part of me was leaving, and as I write I am sure of it. Patti Ann fell asleep crying in the car on the way home and all the children keep saying how much they love you and miss you.
>
> I am doing the best I can without you and so far, we are getting along fine but not the same as when my gal is here.
>
> I sure hope and pray that Grandma [Edna] is getting better for I know that you being there will help a lot. I lit a candle for her in church and with the grace of God, everything will be all right. I want to caution you again on what might happen, and you must take it all in stride and accept what can't be changed.
>
> We seem to be getting along just fine in all departments, a little on the sloppy side but you know how five men get along. Everyone is cooperating from David down to Bobby. I have gone shopping and are stocked for at least a week.
>
> Bobby and Pat Jr. are playing checkers on the floor and they both say to tell Mommy they miss her and love her.
>
> Larry is at the coffee table writing you a letter. David has gone to Confraternity and Patti is watching television (moved back to the living room.)
>
> I seem to have quite a bit of room in bed without being pushed out but I don't like it.
>
> Tell Grandma that we're all thinking of her and praying for fast return to health.
>
> I miss you so very much and love you more than life.
>
> Always and forever,
Your husband
>
> P.S.: It's snowing and the wind is really blowing. Write often.

CHAPTER 5

In an undated letter from around this time, Patsie tells Jeneé some good news: He has found a bigger house for his family.

Dearest,

> *I haven't received any mail from you since Saturday, and it makes me feel so blue. I think of you and the kids constantly and worry about you. It was 96 degrees in the shade today and the humidity is awful high.*
>
> *Honey, I have some good news for you. J.D. Brown and family have found a bigger place and we are to get his place. The real estate man is drawing up the lease and in several days, I am going to sign it. Please let me know when you will arrive because I am going to try to have us moved by the time you get here if it is all possible.*
>
> *I am feeling fine but so lonely. I don't think I can ever consent to your going again for I don't think I can stand it. I love you so very much and hope sometimes to wake up at night with you beside me but to no avail.*
>
> *Maybe you haven't had time to write and are having a good time. Perhaps you are forgetting all about your husband. Please don't. Give my sweethearts a big, big kiss from their Daddy.*
>
> *All my love,*
Your husband
>
> *P.S.: Say hello to the folks and hoping they will come to see us next time.*

A short time later, Patsie repeats in a letter how much he loves Jeneé and how concerned he is for her mother. He tries to ease her mind that he and the kids are fine, and he describes how much he loves his mother-in-law. Patsie also writes about a device he hopes to patent soon—one of the early revelations about his innovation and thirst for making things.

> *My Dearest Doll,*
>
> *I just had to call you today and hear your voice. Mom, I miss you terribly, more than I have ever missed you before. I don't know what it is or why it bothers me so much. All I know is that I do.*
>
> *This morning, Patti did all the vacuuming and made the beds. Larry did the dusting as usual. David painted all the six windows of the basement, and I have ordered aluminum windows from Jaworski for them...*
>
> *I took Larry to the Little League tryout and Patti, Corky and Bobby from 12 o'clock to 5 o'clock. Larry was terrific in comparison to the other 9 year olds. I never realized he was so good a ball player. That kid has more talent than the rest of the family.*
>
> *Bob Wagner the lawyer called and he is trying hard to get the patent ready for us. The new unit I designed works wonderful. I am going to give him the circuit for the new unit Tuesday and he hopes to have the patent pending by sometime in June.*
>
> *Alberta* [Patsie's sister-in-law] *came and took the clothes and ironed them. I didn't know who took the clothes until I saw Alberta bringing them in today. Mrs. Krosky* [a friend] *made us a cake and offered to help in any way...*
>
> *I will pray for your mother's recovery. Tell Grandma that I think the world of her and that she is a wonderful mother-in-law. I like everything about her, especially because she is so very much like me, and I have always understood her. Grandma is extra special with me because she gave me such a wonderful wife who I love more than life.*

CHAPTER 5

Well, Doll, I will stop now but will write more later. The kids all send their love.

Love forever,
Pat

As Edna Hume's health continued to decline, Jeneé realized she needed to stay with her longer. However, it caused considerable stress to continue to worry about her family in Lorain. Patsie, despite being miles away, could sense what was happening. In a letter written shortly before Edna passed away, *[On Patterson-Emerson-Comstock Inc. stationery]*, Patsie told Jeneé how he was continuing to pray for her mother:

Dearest Doll,

I hope this finds you well and you are standing up to all you are going through....Mom, I don't want you to come home if you feel you should stay. I don't want you to feel you didn't do the right thing and let it bother you so much that you might get sick...

I know that your mother doesn't know you anymore but I am thinking about Grandpa. He is probably being optimistic at the present time but when it happens, I don't know how he will feel.

I went to church Sunday and took Holy Communion for your mother. I prayed to God for her throughout the Mass and asked God to let the Communion host that I took be as if it were Grandma taking it. In my rash and abrupt way, I liked Grandma an awful lot.

The kids are fine but they do miss you terribly. May God watch over you for me.

Love forever and ever,
Your husband

Edna Hume died in August 1963. She was buried in Crown Hill Cemetery, in Powell, Wyoming. Jeneé grieved deeply for her loss. But she didn't have much time for bereavement. She attended her mother's funeral on a Thursday, flew back to Lorain on Friday, and went to church for Patsie's sister Rosemary's wedding at 8 a.m. on Saturday.

It was a whirlwind of a week—not too different from a usual week with the Campana family.

But of course, things for the Campana family would take a new turn just a few years later, when Patsie finally put his ideas to the test and dipped his toes into the waters of entrepreneurship.

CHAPTER 6

AN INVENTOR AT HEART

Even before he branched out on his own, Patsie flashed an innovative streak. In fact, when he signed on with Hatfield Electric Co. in 1967, he had already patented his first invention.

Granted a patent on June 21, 1966, Patsie's Emergency Traffic Control System enabled emergency vehicles to turn traffic signals red at intersections, thus stopping traffic so the vehicle could pass safely. His co-inventor was Thomas T. Chrysler, a fellow electrician. The pair formed a corporation called Chrys-Camp Controller Inc. Some of the first municipalities to install the Chrys-Camp system were the Ohio cities of Fairview Park and Bellevue.

The circuitry of the system was quite complex for its time. It used older-style components, as newly-developed transistors were in limited use. And, the system utilized a limited distance radio signal to remotely pre-empt the traffic signals. Similar, yet more sophisticated, systems have since been developed, but the Chrys-Camp system was one of the earliest to be patented. Traffic pre-emption systems are now a standard in cities.

Blessed with an inquisitive mind, Patsie was always intrigued with learning and innovation. He was constantly thinking of more efficient ways to make a product or streamline a process. When he met a person for the first time, the conversation would inevitably turn to what the person did for a living and how he or his company performed the task.

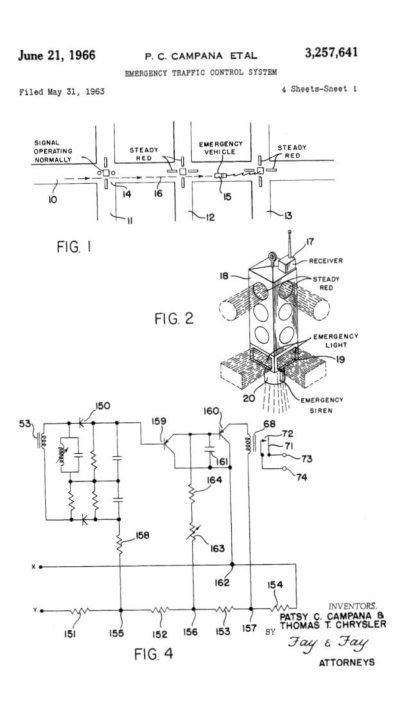

First page of the patent for the emergency traffic control system.

Patent attorney Richard Minnich of Fay Sharpe summed up how critical Patsie's innovation was to his companies. He called Patsie one of the rare and truly unique individuals who can see a problem, visualize a solution, and put that vision into practice to solve the problem.

Minnich worked with Patsie for more than 20 years on patents varying from mechanical principles to complex chemical/metallurgical phenomenon. He said he was always impressed with Patsie's understanding and insight in the underlying principles associated with each project.

"I personally have witnessed many of his ideas being turned into commercial products, which have become the backbone of the various Campana companies," he said. "To say that he was essential to the success of the companies is an understatement. Without him, the companies would not be a fraction of what they are today."

Always thinking, always searching for a better way to do something,

CHAPTER 6

Patsie never called on anyone in a company to do what he was capable of doing himself. Even the natural gas going into his shops was not immune from his tinkering. Instead of buying acetylene to use for the welding and burning process, he found a way to "skin the cat"—to make things a little better and a little cheaper. Patsie was able to compress natural gas so that it would achieve the same result as the more expensive option: buying acetylene in cylinders.

Another example of Patsie's innovation was when he wanted to devise a process to coat steel with certain alloys so it wouldn't rust. He insisted that it not be called "coated;" it was "infused." In his head, this process changed the steel into something else. He was going to make regular steel corrosion-resistant, to the point where it could be used for bridges and rebar for concrete structure, which would not corrode and therefore last longer.

While this particular project never came to fruition, Patsie didn't let the idea go. Giving up was never his decision; and he knew some projects were a gamble. But, he found that stubborn persistence in spite of difficulties could eventually bring success.

Interestingly, Patsie was always generous in sharing the credit for good ideas. For example, the five patents that pertained to welding cast-iron ingot molds were the result of a licensing agreement with a German entrepreneur named Egon Evertz.

Evertz was a flamboyant millionaire, who had been a race car champion in four classes, a concert violinist, a team chess champion, and flew his own 10-passenger jet. Patsie met Evertz through attorney Dick Colella.

The product licensing relationship they forged proved to be one of the most lucrative revenue streams for the company. Together, in a joint venture called CEMCO, Inc., the two entrepreneurs supplied critical steel mill products and services: tubular burning products; new industrial magnets and repair services; slide gate refractories; continuous caster copper tubes and plates for molds; complete mold and segment manufacturing and repair; and slitting, grinding, and scarfing services for slabs, billets and rounds.

With the profitable licensing arrangement, not only did CEMCO, Inc., bring in revenue, it provided momentum for the entire Campana enterprise. From that point on, the sky was the limit.

Entrepreneurial dreamer: Founding P.C. Campana
By the mid-to-late 1960s, life was good for Patsie and the Campana family. Patsie was successful in his work at Hatfield Electric. His ideas around starting his own company were swirling around in his head. And his family was continuing to grow. In 1968, Jeneé was expecting their sixth child, Scotti.

As the story goes, Patsie, then 48, was away on business. He phoned his wife to tell her, "Jeneé, I want to come home to talk to you. I spoke with Stan Pijor [chairman and CEO] at Lorain National Bank, and I have an idea. I want to start a company."

Patsie came home for the weekend. Jeneé made him dinner.

After dinner, he discussed his dream to be an electrical contractor.

Jeneé smiled, got up, left the room, and returned. In her hands, she brought bank books that showed she had secretly been saving money for years. As he looked at the books, Patsie saw that Jeneé had managed to put away an enormous sum of money by using only the bare minimum of Patsie's paychecks for family expenses every month. Patsie had no knowledge of her efforts.

But that was who Jeneé was. Having grown up on a farm with habits of frugality instilled within her from an early age, she raised her family like she was raised: She served meals of ground bologna sandwiches, collected

CHAPTER 6

coupons to save on purchases, and bought used clothing. The children all did chores, and the older ones helped watch the younger ones.

After 22 years of marriage, it turned out that Jeneé had socked away what the Campana children say was at least $50,000, perhaps more. Some speculate that it was possibly twice that amount. And, looking back, if it wasn't for her thriftiness and support, Patsie wouldn't have had the chance to walk away from a well-paying job and launch his own business.

Patsie built a fritter/wiener stand for an expectant Jeneé (their first business together).

So, Patsie began to put his plan in motion. He struck deals with local companies to buy equipment and started to bring in customers from his existing network. On August 26, 1969, the new venture was official. Along with attorneys Ray Miraldi and Dick Colella, P.C. Campana Electric Inc., was formed as an Ohio corporation.

Initially, there were 500 shares and working capital of $500. The company was located at the Campana home, 2614 Sherwood Drive in Lorain—a four-bedroom ranch house that in 1965 Patsie designed and built for his family.

In 1970, the corporation name was changed to P.C. Campana, Inc., to reflect a wider range of services offered, particularly for steel mills, and to allow for future companies under the Campana umbrella. It also marked Patsie's full-time departure from Hatfield Electric to focus full-time on the new company.

A new location quickly followed the name change. Patsie designed and built company offices at 2115 West Park Drive. Originally a one-

77

level building, Patsie would later add a second story. One of his other projects on West Park Drive was the bus garage and office of the Cleveland-Lorain Highway Coach Co. Although it was built for the Sanborn brothers, Patsie later bought it from them.

The P.C. Campana Co. starts to take shape. Patsie, with Patti Ann, Larry and David

While electrical contracting was a company specialty, Patsie didn't let that limit his company's focus. For example, he designed and planned the Koury Building for his good friend, attorney Leo Koury. The office building was built over the site of Koury's burned-down Mill Tavern—and thanks to Patsie's urging, Koury gave it a solid foundation rather than just using the compacted debris, which was unstable and was causing problems settling.

"Patsie gave me the idea to build an office building where my father's saloon used to be, and he was totally honest," Koury said. "He wasn't afraid to give up trade secrets he used. He showed me how he built his building differently than most people build buildings.

"He also used a concrete block that had a rough edge on the outside and was flat on the inside," Koury says. "It was thick enough that he didn't have to insulate and put in Styrofoam, and then he would put on wood siding, which eliminated the unnecessary expense of insulation. "He didn't ask for any money or anything; he volunteered his help—he was such an honest guy."

The electrical contracting business was growing year after year and Patsie continued to build a strong team of professionals to serve the

CHAPTER 6

Greater Cleveland industrial market. Soon after starting the business, Patsie was told of an exciting new opportunity by his attorney Dick Colella. While in Germany on business of his own, Colella met Egon Evertz, a German industrialist. Evertz was a brilliant man who was looking for a North American licensee for his cast iron welding technology and repair process. Colella immediately knew that Patsie was the perfect solution to introduce this technology to steel mills across the United States and Canada, and on October 1, 1974, Evertz and Patsie signed a license agreement.

The cast iron repair solved a persistent problem in the steel industry: Steel mills would have to continually replace expensive ingot molds after they cracked from constant expansion and contraction during the steel-making process. Using this method, it could extend the life of the molds for one-tenth of what it would cost to replace the entire mold.

Word quickly spread about P.C. Campana's cutting edge technology and sales skyrocketed from an annual $1 million to $30 million. Jobsites were set up in steel mills in the United States and Canada to repair ingot molds and slab pots. The savings to the steelmakers were enormous compared to buying new molds and pots.

Profits at P.C. Campana were healthy. The license agreement proved to be a catalyst for Patsie to further expand the company.

David, PC, Pat and Larry.

Chairman of the board and CEO, Patsie sought projects to restore and renovate previously closed factories and department stores. Then he began industrial operations, returning the buildings to productivity—

manufacturing tubing and fabricating steel and other products. By 1975, his company was known throughout the steel industry as the leading supplier of tubular burning products and as one of the top cast iron repair services in the country for ingot molds and slag pots.

In 1975, Patsie created the Caldo Division to produce burning products used at jobsites for cast iron repairs. It was designed to explore how the company could make its own products. As an example, large volumes of welding and burning products were used in the repair of ingot molds, coke oven doors, ladles, slag pots, and industrial equipment. Patsie believed that if the company could manufacture its own products rather than purchase parts from other suppliers, it could produce them more efficiently and ensure quality.

Among the products developed were ones for underwater welding,

THE CALDO TORCH—CUTTING THROUGH ANYTHING MADE EASY

One of Patsie's first fascinations was with welding. This led to one of his earliest patents—the Caldo Torch, a way to cut through any material.

To cut cast iron, welders would use a high-temperature burning bar product. But the bars were expensive, and Patsie felt there had to be a better way. By running steel wires through a tube and connecting them to an oxygen source, he came up with an alternative.

The Caldo Torch in action

Calling it the Italian word for hot—caldo—Patsie designed a lance-type torch in which oxygen flowed under pressure through the lance casing.

The oxygen improved the thermal reaction that occurred when a burning rod was ignited. While the rod was consumed during the process, the Caldo Torch would cut through any material, even concrete.

A later version, the Mini Caldo Torch, soon followed.

CHAPTER 6

concrete cutting, oxygen cutting, lance pipes, and burning bars. And then, there was the Caldo Torch, patented in 1978, and the Caldo Division sales soared.

To secure a site large enough to provide the expanded services the steelmakers would need, in 1979 Patsie bought the Thew Shovel building at 1374 East 28th Street in Lorain. Built in 1898, the structure was closed in 1974 by the Koehring Co., when it moved its facility to the sunbelt. The 300,000 square-foot industrial plant was at Patsie's disposal to further increase services and products. Patsie and plant manager Mike Marsico quickly filled the facilities with fabrication services and manufacturing systems.

The former Thew Shovel building was purchased in 1979.

Several pieces had to come together for the purchase to happen. First, it started with Patsie's inner circle of friends, which included Leo Koury, Karel Fiser and Frank Provenza. Together, they went with Leo's real estate agent brother, Michael Koury, to check out the Thew Shovel site. The group had been watching a football game at Leo's house when Michael told Patsie that he ought to buy the Thew Shovel property.

Patsie answered, "Well, shoot; let's go look at it."

And so, they did. They viewed the 300,000 square feet of empty space, and Patsie liked what he saw, so much so that he immediately proclaimed: "I think I'm going to buy it."

Asked what he would do with it, he said, "I don't know; I'll fill it up."

And that's exactly what he did. Patsie soon filled the building with departments for fabrication and other industry services.

AGAINST ALL ODDS / THE PATSIE CAMPANA STORY

While operations at that location have been downsized since those days, today the Campana company is planning to upgrade and remodel the facilities as part of an improvement project. As a result, Twenty-Eighth Street is going to have a whole new look in the future.

A few years later, in 1984, P.C. Campana opened the Mini Riser Division. It supplied products to the foundry industry, including exothermic sleeves, exothermic risers, exothermic cutting systems, insulating sleeves, mini risers, and hot topping compound.

PAT CAMPANA JR. TAKES OVER THE TUBULAR DIVISION

Patsie learned of a pipe manufacturing plant in Alabama that was for sale. If the plant was a good investment, it might make sense to purchase the plant's equipment, ship it to Lorain, and reassemble the equipment for use in Lorain. Then P.C. Campana would be able to meet its own demands, and those of industry, for tubular products in sizes ranging from ½-inch through 3-inch diameters, as well as rectangles and squares up to 1-½ inches with lengths to 24 feet.

Pat Campana Jr. and Jeneé.

It was about 1980, and Patsie's son Pat Jr. had graduated from Ohio State University with a degree in industrial technology. Patsie put him to work for the company in sales, but after a few months, it was clear it wasn't a good fit.

Patsie had a plan. He wanted to send Pat Jr. to Birmingham, Alabama, to inspect a pipe mill that was for sale. It would be Pat's job to decide if it was worth the asking price of $200,000. Pat took on the challenge willingly, pleased that his father trusted his judgment. The machinery was all in good shape mechanically, so the purchase went through—but there was one more job for Pat. Patsie wanted him to oversee how the equipment was dismantled, shipped, reassembled, and put into operation in Lorain.

The plan to produce their own tubing worked, and it also brought Pat Jr. a promotion: He became the tube mill manufacturing plant manager.

CHAPTER 6

And then, in 1985, the Alloy Cored Wire Division was created after Patsie developed a cored wire system for mixing steelmaking ingredients into the ladle. The system was used to transport and pour out molten metals, that was far superior to other such systems.

Here is a list of locations that are now or have been owned by Patsie and his company:

- The 3000 Leavitt Rd., Amherst, plant measures 109,500 square feet. This is a former Clarkins store, which closed in 1981 and was purchased in 1987. In 1995, the P.C. Campana Industrial Park was developed on the site.
- In 1989, the company purchased another former Clarkins store on Abbe Road in Elyria, measuring 105,000 square feet.
- The Jen-D-Sons plant at East 28th Street and Fulton Avenue in Lorain manufactures tubular products and offers fabrication and packaging services. It has 300,000 square feet of industrial facilities.
- A 1401 South Pine St., Warren, tube mill measured 54,000 square feet.
- The 3725 Grove Ave., Lorain, plant measures 89,500 square feet.
- At 1151 Sunnyside Road. Vermilion, the company has two facilities measuring a total of 85,000 square feet.
- Other locations included Schererville, Indiana; Baltimore, Maryland; Chicago, Illinois.; and Michigan City, Indiana.
- A number of jobsites are located inside steel mills across the United States and Canada.
- Corporate offices are currently located at 6155 Park Square Drive in Lorain.

An early photo of the corporate building

ALLOY CORED WIRE—ANOTHER WAY TO IMPROVE A PROCESS

Alloy cored wire, along with its drive equipment, was one of the first products to make a name for the company. Today, P.C. Campana remains one of the major producers of cored wire in the world.

One of the ways to understand the role alloy cored wire plays in steel making is to compare the process to making a pot of soup or a milkshake.

While soup contains seasonings readily available from a grocery store, in the steel industry, the source is the periodic table of elements. This often involves manganese, sulfur, titanium, and cobalt.

Likewise, a milkshake starts out with vanilla ice cream. And then, strawberries or chocolate syrup are added.

Imagine that all those ingredients are inside a wire. You add the wire to the vat of molten material, according to the recipe, and the steel comes out perfect every time.

Before cored wire came on the scene, steelmakers dumped the ingredients into ladles using shovels or bags of material. However, it was difficult to mix the ingredients below the layer of slag on the top (slag is basically lime and impurities, the magic of steelmaking is performed underneath that layer). At the bottom is a layer of argon that would help stir the steel to mix it up.

Cored wire can penetrate the thick concoction. It seeps down into the hot metal, so when every ingredient dissolves, and then is mixed, it creates the steel with optimum results.

P.C. Campana learned about this material in 1981 during a trip to Europe—it had been invented by a company named Valvorec. The material was in a ribbon shape, but it had an occasional tendency to open, which was undesirable. This opening occurred because of the way the material was mechanically sealed.

It was out of this observation that alloy cored round wire came to be. P.C. Campana was soon perfecting the wire by electric welding it first.

CHAPTER 6

But some complaints quickly arose about a flaw in the process; customers wanted proof that the additives were properly inside the cored wire. Patsie turned to his friend and business partner, Al Hillegass, for help.

"I know this process is better than the twist process as far as getting the material down into the vat," Patsie said, "because it's together longer."

He asked Hillegass to have his chief metallurgist put together a study showing that the cored wire was superior to other products.

There were two problems. First, the product was stiff and unruly and customers didn't like that. Second, there was a heating flaw because the welded wire wasn't pulling down into the vat.

Hillegass proposed that Patsie return to the twisted design process. Once that was done, Patsie added a programmable feeding mechanism to automatically inject the wire to ensure the desired specifications. Soon the company launched a line of wire feeders to insert the cored wire into the ladle at speeds of 600-to-1,000 feet per minute. Hundreds of these machines are now in use in North America.

Despite his travels and various ventures deep in the heart of Texas, Patsie always wanted his home base to be in Lorain. He purchased sites in other cities, but his heart was in Lorain. And, he made a point of getting involved in the city and its civic organizations.

Over the years, Patsie was a member of the International Brotherhood of Electrical Workers, the National Electrical Contractors Association, the American Institute of Metallurgical Engineers, and the American Institute of Steel Engineers.

He served on the board of directors of Lorain National Bank, was chairman of the Industrial Task Force for the City of Lorain, was a member of the city planning commission and board of zoning appeals, and in the late 1970s served on the Lorain Port Authority.

One of Patsie's long-term dreams was to buy the American Ship Building Co.'s Lorain Yard, which was closed in 1984 by company owner George Steinbrenner following labor union turmoil.

AGAINST ALL ODDS / THE PATSIE CAMPANA STORY

WHAT'S IN A NAME? LOOK CLOSELY, AND YOU'LL SEE

Patsie Campana valued family and friends. As P.C. Campana grew and specialty areas were developed, Patsie wanted to honor them when it came time to name the divisions.

One of the earliest corporations was CEMCO Inc., formed in 1971 from the names of Campana, Evertz, Miraldi, and Colella. Egon Evertz, entrepreneur, and Ray Miraldi and Dick Colella, Patsie's attorneys, were partners in the venture, which dealt with cast iron ingot repairs and other foundry services.

A non-ethnic touch in naming was Bell Service Systems Inc., but the meaning, if you knew Italian, was clear; "campana" translates to "bell." The company was incorporated in 1975 to engage in steel mill services and systems.

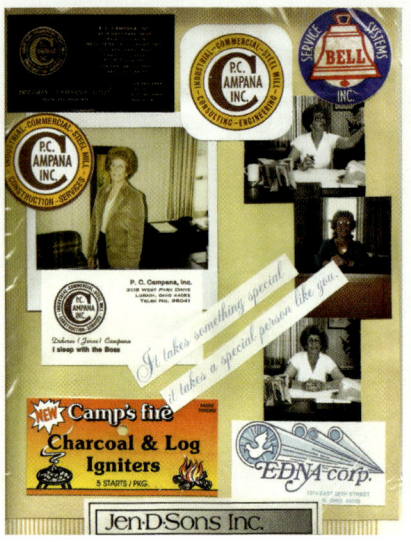

Campana company logos over the years, along with Jeneé's business card as secretary/treasurer of the corporation.

In the late 1970s, the company bought a plant in Vermilion to conduct coke oven door repair and mold repair for steel mills and foundries, as well as fabricating work. It was named Jen-D-Sons Inc., after Jeneé, daughter, and sons, and the name also gave it a non-ethnic touch.

Jeneé's mother Edna Hume was honored when Edna Corp. was created in 1981 to specialize in tubular steel manufacture, fabricating, and sales.

Not to ignore Patsie's own mother, Maria Nicole, Inc., was created in the mid-1980s. It is a corporation formed to own and hold securities issued by other companies.

In 1987, Camp-Hill, Inc., was founded, the name a combination of partners Patsie Campana and Al Hillegass. Eventually, Camp-Hill operated three steel mill plants and improved them where the previous owners couldn't.

CHAPTER 6

Patsie was acquainted with Steinbrenner as he was a regular customer at The Castle on the Lake restaurant in Lorain. It was there he also met businessman Alan Spitzer, whose family auto dealerships would become an empire in the region.

Both Patsie and Spitzer submitted bids for the shipyards, but Steinbrenner accepted Spitzer's bid over Patsie's. Spitzer developed the site into the HarborWalk condos and marina on the Black River.

This didn't sit well with Patsie. He wanted to keep the shipyard going to employ repair workers for Great Lakes ships, and so that the city of Lorain would maintain tax revenue.

Patsie believed in Lorain, and thought it an unfortunate waste to use the city's unique access to Lake Erie just to put condos on the beautiful industrial property.

In 2000, several years after Patsie's death, then-Lorain Mayor Craig Foltin named a city park after Patsie. Called Campana Park and located at West Park Drive and Meister Road, today it offers 11 baseball/softball fields, as well as soccer fields and basketball courts. There are also playgrounds, grills, and picnic tables. The Pipe Yard Stadium, located there, is the home of the Lorain County Ironmen, a Great Lakes Summer Collegiate League baseball team.

Supporters of the late greeting card poet and Lorain native Helen Steiner Rice had asked that the park be named for her. But the mayor rejected the request since she had spent most of her life in Cincinnati, not Lorain.

"Campana made the choice to make Lorain his home while others chose to go to other places," Foltin told the Associated Press. "As much as I admire Ms. Rice, I think if we were going to do something for her, we'd have to look at Toni Morrison—Lorain's most famous writer—too."

As the years went by and Patsie's company became more successful, he codified a number of ideas he believed had become underpinnings to his ability to growth and thrive. These five major principles eventually became the P.C. Campana guidelines for success:

1. **Always promote from within.** The company's top managers all worked on the shop floor. The policy encouraged employees to strive for promotions.
2. **Share the wealth.** A profit-sharing plan was instituted to allow workers to share in the company's success. In addition, workers are rewarded for suggestions.
3. **Make the workplace as fun and casual as possible.** Casual dress is encouraged for managers and employees. First names are preferred, rather than "Mr. Campana."
4. **Help make employees feel included.** By keeping employees informed about company decisions, they stay interested in the company and its direction.
5. **Allow managers to make decisions.** By empowering managers to run their own operations and be accountable for their actions, they will teach employees their roles and employees will understand their investment in the company's success.

CHAPTER 7

CROSSED PATHS: HOW A RELATIONSHIP WITH A VETERAN STEEL EXECUTIVE LED TO SUCCESSFUL BUSINESS VENTURES

By the early 1970s, while Patsie was building his enterprise, his path was destined to cross with another man that was on a similar journey—Al Hillegass. Their future association would soon become something both men would treasure as business associates and friends for the rest of their lives.

Hillegass began working for United States Steel in 1949 at a Pittsburgh location. He climbed the executive ladder and, by 1972, was promoted to division superintendent of the rolling mills at the Lorain Works.

Two new bar mills had been installed at this site, but unfortunately, the bar mills didn't get off to a good start. Hillegass was called in to resolve the problem. He oversaw some quick improvements, and all was going well until a discovery: the mills were only producing half of their necessary output because of electrical problems. The grinding machines, an integral part of the bar mills' process, were constantly stalling due to electrical shorts. This was creating costly delays.

"We had to do something about the grinders; this was very important," Hillegass said. "The engineering department decided that we could move the electrical feed lines topside, out of the pits where they were, and that was going to be about a million-dollar job at the time."

The work was estimated to take a week, and time was of the essence; the plant wouldn't be producing anything for seven days. That would be seven days of lost profits in addition to the million-dollar loss of the actual job.

Three firms bid on the job—two large companies and Patsie's fledgling business.

"So, the man in charge of the rolling mill told me, 'I think we're going to give it to the Campana group,'" Hillegass said. "I asked, 'Are you sure we want to do that?' and he said, 'Well, he's the lowest bidder, and I think he's anxious to get the job. He'll do it.' I said, 'Well, bring him in here so we can talk to him before we do this.'"

It was Hillegass' first introduction to Patsie. He had heard about him and his company before, but the two had never met. Hillegass recounts the story of their first encounter:

> I told Patsie, 'You have to understand, we have to get it done in a week, and it has to be able to operate properly.' He said, 'It will do that.' And he kept telling me, 'We'll be able to do that.' Finally, I asked, 'Well, what if you don't do it?' and Patsie said, 'I'm telling you; we're going to do it.'
>
> That did little to reassure me and I stated, 'Well, other people would give financial assurance and a backup plan if they can't get it done and so forth.'
>
> He said, 'I don't do that; I just give you my word. Look, Mr. Hillegass; I personally guarantee you we will get that job done to your satisfaction in time, and it will work, OK?'
>
> So, I gave him the job. He finished it 12 hours before the week was up.
>
> The timing concern taken care of, the next question was if it would work—and it did. The maintenance supervisor told me, 'Man, the line is working great now.'
>
> From that point on, the plant was able to put out the required materials at the proper rate, and that made everybody happy.

CHAPTER 7

About a month later, the maintenance superintendent told me that Patsie wanted to see him.

I said, 'Tell him we're happy with the job, you know, and he's been paid, so that isn't necessary.'

But Patsie was insistent.

I was thinking that perhaps the job was going to cost more money than had been estimated.

We were sitting in my office, and Patsie asked, 'So, how did you like the job?'

I said, 'Well, Pete'—that was my maintenance guy—'told you we're very delighted; it's working fine.'

'Well, I'm glad. I'm a man of my word, aren't I?' Patsie said.

'Yep,' I replied; I was waiting for the next shoe to drop.

Patsie finally said, 'Well, I've got something for you.'

He gave me a check for $50,000, made out to U.S. Steel–Lorain.

Patsie explained that his company did better than he estimated. 'Actually, we did $100,000 less, and I'm sharing half of that with you guys.'

But I didn't want a check; a deal was a deal.

'No, no, no, no, no,' Patsie said, 'I insist that you take this check.'

I finally accepted it and submitted it to the accounting department, explaining that it was a rebate from the job.

The accountant said, 'We've never had one of those before. You know, it'll cause more trouble than it's worth; for instance, what are we getting this back for?'

So, the check was never cashed; it was torn up.

Later, when Patsie and I became close friends, I brought up the check matter.

'You know what happened?' I asked.

Patsie said, 'Yeah; you guys didn't cash it.'

91

> *I acknowledged that it was destroyed.*
> *'That's too bad, isn't it? I knew you wouldn't take it,'*
> *Patsie said.*
> *That's what he said—he knew we wouldn't take it.*
> *He said, 'It just makes good advertising.'*

This incident featured all the elements to make it a classic Patsie story: competitive pricing, an ambitious timetable, and superior customer service.

After a while, Hillegass was transferred back to the Pittsburgh area. A few years later, in 1976, he was eventually reassigned to the Lorain Works to serve as general superintendent. Hillegass looked up Patsie, and the two men resumed their friendship as though it had never stopped.

"That's when I picked up with Patsie, not so much on the business side, but on the friendship side. I liked him," Hillegass said. "We did some things together socially. I met his wife and became friends with Jeneé. But the electrical project was the last business experience I had with him until I left U.S. Steel in 1982."

Within a few years, Hillegass rose to company group president. But, he wanted to retire early from U.S. Steel as he had plans to strike out on his own and open a steel mill in Arkansas—an estimated $500 million steel mill/pipe mill project. So, he asked Patsie for his input.

Patsie, valuing the friendship highly, estimated the construction of the entire project for the bank financing free of charge for Hillegass. But the nation was in a recession then, interest rates soared to 21 percent, oil plummeted to $10 a barrel, and Hillegass called the project off.

He thanked Patsie for all the work he did, and the ever humble Patsie replied, "Al, don't worry about it. If you ever get an opportunity, just think of me."

A few years later, Hillegass called and said, "Hey, Pat, I've got an opportunity," and thus began a partnership in out-of-state pipe mills.

With his connections and experience, Hillegass had learned how U.S.

CHAPTER 7

Steel was interested in restarting a steel mill it had previously shut down in McKeesport, Pennsylvania, formerly called the National Works. It was the mill where Hillegass had first started working with U.S. Steel many years earlier. He saw an opportunity, and contacted Patsie to see if he would invest in the project.

The Camp-Hill complex.

Patsie liked what he heard. The two men formed Camp-Hill Corp. in 1987, using a combination of their two names to christen the venture. Negotiations began that summer with U.S. Steel, and by the following year, the mill was up and running.

The first pipe was produced February 2, 1988, recalled Karen Trautwein, P.C. Campana's corporate administrator.

Patsie assigned Trautwein to bring the Camp-Hill office up to speed on the new venture. The employees were former U.S. Steel employees.

"We needed to get the office set up," Trautwein recalled. "With me being neutral and not being a Campana, Patsie brought me in because he trusted me, and he knew that I would never, ever lie to him or whatever. He wanted to set up the office the way our office was set up, so I went to Camp-Hill, and I spent a lot of time getting it organized and getting good people to work with. And Al Hillegass learned to trust me too."

Patsie invested $500,000. Within a year, Camp-Hill had paid him back.

"He was really happy with that," Hillegass said. "He said, 'That's one of the best investments I ever made.' I said, 'Well, it is good for me, too.'"

Camp-Hill operated the mill for the next 27 years. Because of Hillegass' foresight and Patsie's experience and perseverance, the pair overcame the odds to take what U.S. Steel thought was a losing proposition and transformed it into a success. They generated more than $50 million in profit and produced more than 4 million tons of pipe.

Camp-Hill takes over the former National Works of U.S. Steel.

In 2009, a new group of U.S. Steel managers began working with Camp-Hill and decided they wanted to pursue production of 20-inch pipe for which the mill was not designed. After exhaustive efforts to produce 20-inch high strength pipe, Camp-Hill management notified U.S. Steel that it was not feasible to do so profitably.

As a result, in May 2011, U.S. Steel ended the contract with Camp-Hill and took over operations at the mill. It ran until August 2014, when profitability concerns caused U.S. Steel to shut down the plant. (In January 2017, the site was purchased by Dura-Bond Industries of Export, Pennsylvania. Dura-Bond announced plans to reopen that mill later in the year. Ironically, Camp-Hill's former president Doug Nolfi was hired to run the plant for Dura-Bond since he was a proven talent for many years while working with Patsie and Al).

Over its years in operation, Patsie and Al undertook two other Camp-Hill steel mill projects: one in Houston, Texas, named Delta

Tubular Processing and the other in Bellville, Texas, named Bellville Tube Corp.

Camp Hill Corporation
Feb 2, 1988 – April 30, 2011
Over 3 Million
Tons of Quality Pipe Produced

Texas operations offer healthy profits...and good memories
Patsie's partnership with Al Hillegass through Camp-Hill was highly successfully from its inception through its dissolution. One of its more memorable ventures began in 1989, when the two men pursued an opportunity in Texas with a tubular steel company named Interlock Technologies Corp.

At the time, Camp-Hill's joint venture with U.S. Steel (then called USX) in McKeesport, Pennsylvania, was delivering strong results. Both Patsie and Al were open to other ideas, and this new opportunity in Texas with Interlock Technologies offered the pair access to another market—the oil and gas drilling industry.

Interlock had a tubular finishing plant in Houston which took seamless pipe and drill casing, which was already manufactured, put threads and couplings on them, and then heat-treated it. Seeing its potential, Camp-Hill acquired the plant, called Delta Tubular Processing, for $10.5 million.

Then, Hillegass and Patsie reached out to U.S. Steel, which was already pleased with its existing partnership with the men, and asked them to market the products for Camp-Hill.

U.S. Steel agreed.

"U.S. Steel decided to be our partner in that, which was good news and bad news, because they had a couple of members on the board, and we had a couple on the board," Hillegass recalled. "U.S. Steel had made great promises on the amount of product they were going to put through there, and they never really reached the target levels.

"So that plant—although it paid all its bills and made a little profit—wasn't a money producer like the McKeesport plant," he said. "But we hung on, and I kept telling them, 'We need to put more volume in there.' We were struggling just like the previous owner was, except we were at least covering the debt."

Running the organization was its own adventure: Patsie would attend the board meetings, Hillegass recalled, and would sit for about 20 minutes and then turn to Al and say, "Al, you handle this; I'm going out in the plant and see what I can do out there. Find out what they need."

That casual arrangement worked as it played to each of the men's strengths.

And, because Patsie had access to the P.C. Campana facilities, he could fabricate whatever might be needed to improve the product output at Delta. This was a win-win, because while it was good business for him, it allowed Delta to increase capacity.

As it turned out, four years into Camp-Hill's ownership of the Delta plant, U.S. Steel wasn't sending nearly as much pipe for processing as originally anticipated. Much of this was due to Patsie's process improvements through his access to P.C. Campana's technology—which had created a larger processing capacity than when Camp-Hill had bought the company and when they had entered into the deal with U.S. Steel. But, it meant that in 1992, Delta was operating at only one-third of its potential capacity.

Both Patsie and Hillegass set out in search of ideas for more business opportunities, and in 1993, Hillegass took a call from Carl Pfeiffer, the CEO of Quanex Corp., a pipe-producing company with a plant in Bellville, Texas.

Pfeiffer asked him, "Would you have any interest in buying that plant?"

CHAPTER 7

Bellville was approximately 60 miles west of Houston, and Pfeiffer recognized it could fit nicely with the Delta plant and what the Camp-Hill group was engaged in through their Texas ventures. He invited Hillegass to meet and look at the plant.

Hillegass agreed. The plant, he learned, was only about seven years old. It was running just one shift, which Hillegass thought wasn't very well operated. The two men continued conversations about the Bellville plant over martinis—and Hillegass learned just how badly Pfeiffer wanted to sell it.

"They had spent $60 million on this place," Hillegass said. "So, we offered them $10 million. They took it."

But there was still one more hurdle—Al had to call Patsie and discuss putting the money together to make the acquisition.

The two men discussed it. It worked out that $3 million of capital was contributed and bank financing was provided by Society Bank (now KeyCorp) for $9.5 million.

Bellville saw immediate results under Camp-Hill management. One of the first ideas Patsie and Al implemented was to send the pipe manufactured at Bellville to Delta for processing. This solved two problems at once: Bellville increased production output and Delta received enough pipe to process to close the gap on its capacity.

Next, Patsie and Hillegass struck a deal with Lone Star Steel to convert their coil steel into pipe on a conversion contract.

"They said, 'Well, give us the costs and your fees,'" Hillegass recalled. "I made a nice, generous offer for the fees, gave it to them and they said, 'When can we start?' So between what we were doing and what they were doing, we managed to fill up Bellville, which really was great, and we were also finishing a lot of tubes at Delta."

Patsie and Al Hillegass celebrate the first load of Bellville pipe.

On April 15, 1993, the first load of pipe came out of Bellville Tube. It was a very happy day for Patsie and Al. But Patsie was only able to enjoy the success at Bellville a short time. He passed away seven months later, on November 24, 1993.

Hillegass recalls how sad it was when Patsie died, and he soon realized that the loss of his partner was unfortunate for Camp-Hill.

"We had the McKeesport plant, it was operating very, very well," he said. "It was a big success from the beginning. But the other two had problems with equipment and management."

His fear was that after Patsie passed away, the children all assumed equal shares of Patsie's Camp-Hill partnership.

"Oh my gosh, who is going to represent the Campana side?" Hillegass thought, "I didn't know if I was going to deal with six kids or what. But Bobby Campana surfaced, and it was a blessing because he was just as much help, not necessarily in the same category as Patsie but in the operation and financial end of the two projects that weren't operating very well."

Bobby and Al worked hard on the problems and one after another they resolved them. Management changes were made at both sites and equipment modifications were made.

CHAPTER 7

Bob and Al Hillegass kept Camp-Hill running after Patsie's death.

"And we did that successfully. So even though I lost a good partner in Patsie, I gained a very good partner in Bobby," Hillegass said. "Not only did we become partners in Camp-Hill with his representing the Campana family, we became lifelong friends.

So despite the loss of Patsie, Bellville Tube and Delta Tubular lived on. Bellville was under the expert guidance of plant manager Ken Beil and Delta was led by a most capable plant manager Jim Bogar. Both plants produced/processed more than 100,000 tons of pipe each year.

Then in 2000, Camp-Hill sold the Bellville plant to Lone Star Steel. Delta Tubular was sold to U.S. Steel in 2003. Both exits were very profitable for Camp-Hill.

At the time of the Bellville sale, Camp-Hill took out a full-page ad in The Bellville Times carrying a thank-you message to the workers and the city.

Thank You, Bellville, for All That You've Done
Thank you, Bellville, for all that you've done.

It was a great experience and a lot of fun.
Patsie and Al took over in 1993.
Isn't it amazing what they could see?
People coming together as a team,
Allowing everyone to share in their dream.

Thank you, Bellville, for making your mark.
It wasn't always a walk in the park.
Market conditions went up and down,
But we always believed in the people of this fine town.
It's you, the people, who made us world-class.
There is no requirement you didn't pass.

Thank you, Bellville, for becoming our friends.
We are hopeful the relationship never ends.
Somehow, we found you in your big state.
Don't you think it had to be fate?
Moving forward we wish you the best.
We hope you invite us back as your guest.

The Campana and Hillegass Families
Bob Campana
Al Hillegass
4/15/93 – 3/31/00

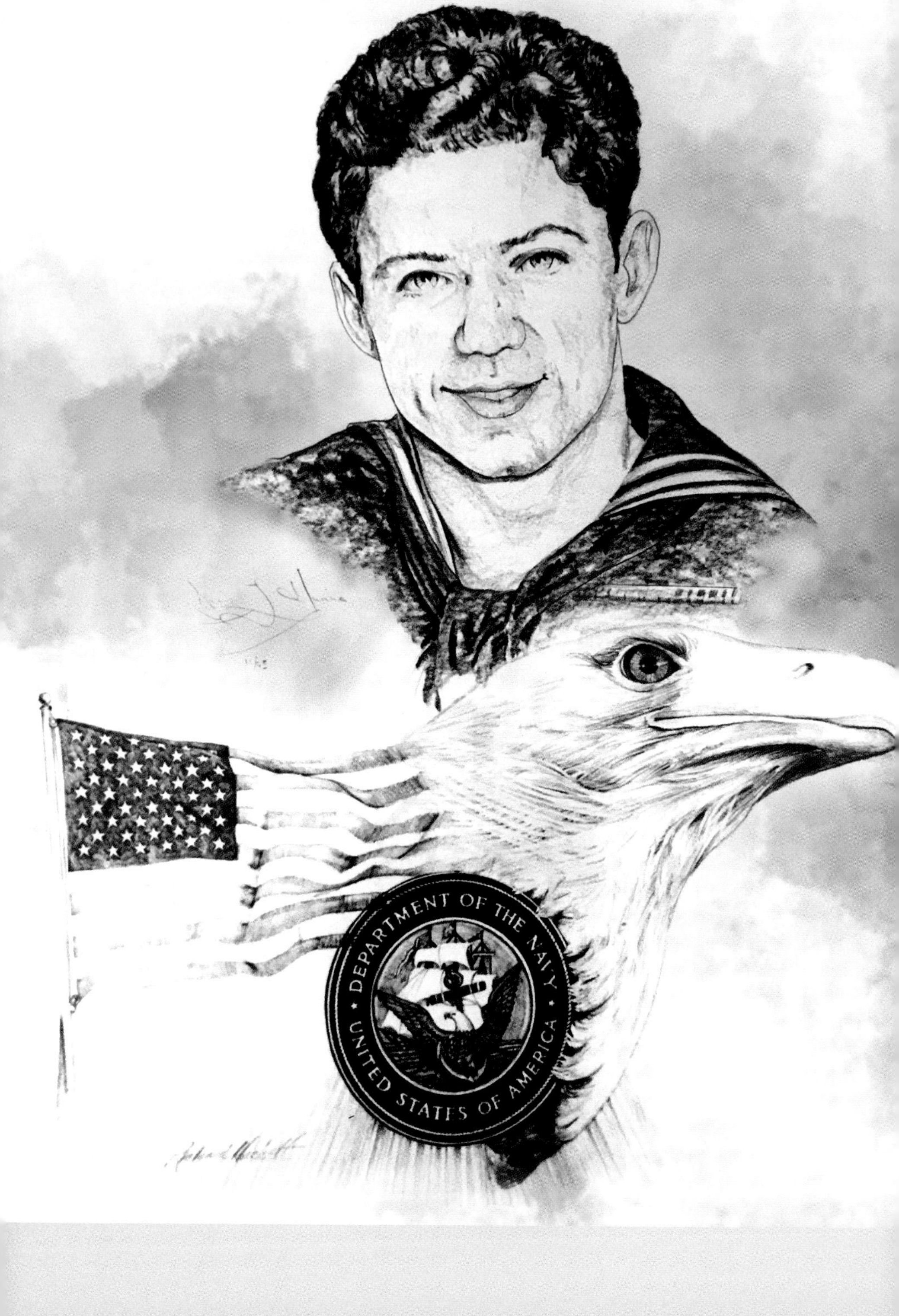
DEPARTMENT OF THE NAVY
UNITED STATES OF AMERICA

PART THREE

PATSIE, THE MAN

CHAPTER 8

VICTORIES OVER HEALTH ISSUES

Over his lifetime, Patsie faced his fair share of health issues—though one might think he had been blessed with nine lives after learning all that he went through.

He was just a preschooler when he dashed in front of a circus wagon and survived a fractured skull and broken bones, which eventually healed over a long and painful recovery period. But, that wasn't his only brush with serious accidents or putting himself in potential harm's way.

A veteran motorcyclist for years—he could drive large Indians and Harley-Davidsons—Patsie never lost his passion for them, even well into his 70s. Once, after seeing the latest and greatest Harley in his golden years, Patsie asked his son Pat Jr. to buy him one.

Patsie was so excited when he got it that he hopped on board and zipped off to Cedar Point, where the family had a cottage on The Chaussee—the highway which led to the amusement park.

At the time, a new restaurant called Shooters had just opened on the harbor. Patsie stopped there to get a bite to eat.

Shooters had a newly installed asphalt parking lot, and after Patsie got off the motorcycle and put its kickstand down, it immediately sunk into the new asphalt.

The motorcycle then fell with a sudden crash, landing on Patsie's leg. The Harley weighed nearly 800 pounds. Its exhaust pipe was so hot from Patsie's long trip that it began to burn his leg. By the time help arrived to pull the motorcycle off him, Patsie's leg had sustained serious burns.

In time, Patsie recovered, but he was not happy about the experience— nor the recovery method. To fix his leg, doctors performed a skin graft procedure. And, to secure enough skin to replace the injured area, they had to take it from his buttocks. Patsie felt that added insult to his injury. And, as it that weren't bad enough, for a long time after the accident, it was difficult for Patsie to either stand or sit.

During his time in the Navy, Patsie acquired a good number of nicks, cuts and bruises, but nothing too serious. And, despite the danger he went through welding metals (both in the Navy and with his different companies), the major accidents were few and far between. Sometimes, Patsie welded in a sport coat or suit, as the occasion presented itself. This presented its own challenges.

So, despite not leading a fit lifestyle, Patsie remained a robust and mostly healthy individual for much of his life.

He bowled and played golf. But the latter sport was curtailed when he injured his back tripping on a railway track as he walked around the company premises.

Patsie's attorney, Dick Colella, once suggested Patsie see an elderly doctor in Vermilion who practiced chiropractic medicine, but actually was an osteopath. The doctor had an old adjustment table in his garage, and Colella had seen him for neck problems, which were successfully treated.

So, Patsie went to Vermilion, and the doctor fixed his back problems. Patsie was so happy that as a token of his appreciation, he rebuilt the doctor's garage.

In the late 1960s or early 1970s, Patsie underwent surgery for a kidney stone that would not pass. His kidney was reversed in position, and the surgery involved a large incision in his torso. Once again, it was something he truly didn't enjoy.

CHAPTER 8

Coincidentally, when Patsie was interviewing Jerry Janasko for an electrical engineer position at P.C. Campana, Janasko mentioned he recently had been hospitalized.

"You just got out of the hospital? What'd you have?" Patsie asked.

"Well, I had a kidney stone; I had a reversed kidney. They couldn't get the stone out, so they cut me in half to get to it," Janasko said.

"And he says, 'I've got the same thing. Look; I am cut in half. Now we're even,'" Janasko recalled.

"So, when I started, he told everybody at the plant, 'Now, I don't want Janasko picking up anything but a pencil. If you see him pick up anything more than a pencil, you stop him or I'll stop you.'"

At his 60th birthday party, Patsie joked with son Bobby.

In 1980, at his 60th birthday party, Patsie was caught on video, daydreaming.

When he saw that the camera was zooming in on him, he smiled and was asked, "What were you thinking about?"

"You know, I will tell you," he said to Bobby, "if you get to be 60 years old and are feeling as good as I feel, you will be lucky. I don't have any problems; maybe a little high blood pressure, but not any problems."

Patsie kept up his busy work schedule, traveling and running the ship, right until his unfortunate passing.

JENEÉ'S LETTER TO P.C. FOR HIS 60TH BIRTHDAY

Pat, today is your 60th birthday, and I can't believe that 37 years have flew by so fast. What a beautiful life I've had because of you. Remember the Cresent ballroom? The hours we would dance? When I'd come home from work you'd be waiting every nite for me. The day you left for sea diving school I thought my whole world had ended, watching the train pull away...

The morn of Dec. 29, 1945, you came back from 26 months overseas. I was in bed and my mom called, "Sis, come down stairs, there is someone here to see you." I ran down with a new white chenille robe on and there stood my handsome man in his sailor suit. I wrecked it hugging you so much that you spent hours cleaning it again.

How we celebrated New Year's Eve '46 on the train going to Lorain for me to meet the Campana family. Then the extended two more months leave that you spent at my folk's house we were together every minute. How we planned for June 8th 1946, when we would become one. The day we moved into our own apartment and there was just the two of us... What a bad cook I was at first, but you always told me everything was good. Then how excited we were when I was P.G. & on Febr. 1, 1948, David was born then 21 months later, Nov. 21th 1949, Patty.

The day we moved to Johnstown, Pa....How hard you worked, I think you went down to 128# and always for your family never once did you ever complain about anything....Then on to Phila and the apt. on Rosevely Blvd., then later to Lott Ave. where #3 Larry was born there. Also, you worked such long hours; but when you weren't working you were with the kids and I always. Our move to Detroit, the beautiful home you bought us & you worked so hard doing the Rec. room & we never even got to use it, because you got a call one Sunday nite to be in Weirton, West Va. the next day to start a new job and we were there 3½ yrs where two more of our children were born, Corky & Bob.

The day you left for Italy for 9½ weeks I thought all my strength had left my body, oh how I missed you, you'll never know...

CHAPTER 8

My big move to Lorain with our 5 beautiful children, the Duplex on New Mexico all I did was write letters every day & pray for your safe return, and the day Rosemary & I came to the airport when you came home from Italy when I saw you get off that plane I'll never be able to tell you how I felt my man was home...

How fast you found a house & we moved to 1138 West 19th St. The day we moved into this house that you built, planned the floor plan and did most of the house, I loved it then I love it now I never, ever want to move. The day #6, Scott was born. Oh God is so good to us 5 handsome son's and one beautiful daughter that are all so good and respectful. And 5 beautiful strong grandchildren, Mark, Kris, Jenee, Rocky and Little Larry. I pray we have many more to carry on your name, you've worked so hard all your life for just me and the kids I know and all I can say Pat is I know I have the greatest MAN on earth, your my friend, my lover, my provider your my everything you've made me so happy.

CHAPTER 9

A SECRET PHILANTHROPIST

If there was one thing Patsie wanted to avoid during his lifetime, it was recognition for his generosity. He recognized he had overcome the odds to become successful. And, he understood that when you become successful, you pay it forward by giving back to those who need it. So, it should come as little surprise that throughout his life, Patsie donated to a countless number of those in need. But, he preferred receiving no recognition for his philanthropy—making it difficult to really know the full depth and breadth of his kindness.

Patsie's nature was one that embraced generosity and sharing, and it manifested itself at an early age. While he had failed first grade because he only understood Italian, Patsie soon mastered English. Once he was proficient in his second language, he began teaching other Italian-heritage children in the neighborhood how to speak English.

Many of them came to Patsie's children throughout the years and said, "Oh, my God. I remember when your dad taught me to speak English."

The bulk of the Italian community lived in one area of Lorain, spread across three streets. The kids would play together, which is how Patsie formed close relationships with them. Soon, he was developing skills in leadership and teaching others what he knew.

Patsie and Dick Colella worked together since the 1960s.

One day, later in his career, Patsie was having dinner at a Bob Evans with his attorney, Dick Colella. At the time, smoking was allowed in restaurants. Patsie was finishing a cigarette when an elderly woman came up to him. Wheeling an oxygen tank to which a tube was connected to help her breathe, she berated Patsie for smoking.

"Stop that; stop it immediately!" she said. "It's hurting me, and more importantly, it's hurting you, and you should know better."

Patsie was appalled.

Colella played it cool. He had already given up smoking and silently agreed the woman was right.

Patsie asked Colella if he could subtly follow the woman out to the parking lot. "Can you go out and see how she got here?" he said.

"What do you mean?" Colella answered.

"What did she come in? Did she come in a truck or van?"

Colella followed her and discovered she had arrived in a van with a handicapped permit. He told Patsie what he had found.

"I don't know, but I think he ended up doing something for her," Colella said. "I was never able to confirm that, but that's how his philanthropy expressed itself."

CHAPTER 9

Chances are, Patsie bought her a new vehicle. He did things like that—quietly, and anonymously.

A similar story involved a young girl in a wheelchair.

Once, when the Campana family was at a cookout, Patsie was in the backyard.

He was gazing out into the distance as other people talked. As it turned out, Patsie was actually looking three yards over, to where a girl was sitting in a wheelchair.

He was captivated by her.

Patsie turned to his son Scotti. "You see that little girl there?" he said. "You know how blessed and lucky you are that you don't have to do that?"

Scotti agreed that it would be tough, and understood that this was a teaching moment.

When the family drove away from the cookout, Patsie slowed down by the house where the girl lived and told Jeneé to remind him about the girl.

Later, he sent workers from P.C. Campana to build a ramp in front of her house.

And, as if that weren't enough, he soon learned the girl needed a $2,600 wheelchair.

Patsie ordered it for her and had it delivered to her house.

Another time, Patsie went to Mike Marsico's office on a Monday morning.

He asked, "Do you know that church near 20th Street and Reed Avenue?"

Marsico acknowledged he knew it.

"I want air conditioning installed in that church, and I don't want nobody to know," Patsie said.

Earlier, the church had invited him to a worship service. Patsie had attended and decided it was so hot in the building that he would install air conditioning—anonymously.

"But that's the way he was; he didn't want any recognition, he didn't want any advertisements," Marsico said. "We also were never allowed to enter into a government contract, because once you get involved with the government, they get their nose in your business and Patsie wouldn't let us do that."

Many of the donations Patsie made were in cash—which helped Patsie retain his anonymity.

Once, he and Jeneé donated 24 jackets to St. Peter's Church so the ushers would all share a common style of sport coat. Another time, they donated shrubbery to the city of Lorain to plant throughout the city.

"Karen, get me $20,000," he on occasion would tell Karen Trautwein, office administrator. And she would go to the bank for the cash, never knowing its destination.

Sometime later, Patsie devised an idea to show how much he appreciated her role in the office. He figured out a way to have her buy herself a gift.

"It was kind of funny," she recalled. "Patsie kept telling me that Jeneé's credit card was not working all the time; Jeneé was having a hard time. He had it in his hand and said, 'I want you to take this card to the store, buy several things, and see if you have a problem with it.'

"So, I took it to a store, bought some office supplies, returned to the office, and told Patsie I didn't have any problem; it worked fine. When I told him I bought office supplies, he said, 'I didn't want you to buy stuff for the office; I wanted you to buy something for yourself!'

"Well, I didn't need anything," she told him. So, the thought was there, even though the plan didn't quite work.

Patsie's philanthropy did have some commonalities—it usually manifested itself from some experience he had with the recipient.

For example, he had a friend named Rich Stammitti. One day, he drove past Rich walking to his job at the Lorain steel mill. Rich was the father of current Lorain County Sheriff, Phil Stammitti (who was a child at the time, one of nine in the family). Patsie had known Rich for a long time.

"Hey, Dicky, what are you doing? Let me give you a ride," Patsie called out to him.

CHAPTER 9

Stammitti got in the car, and Patsie started driving around.

They picked up some lunch and were talking. Patsie found out that Stammitti couldn't pay to get his car repaired, and that's why he was walking to work.

Patsie later pulled up to Stammitti's driveway in a 1955 Buick and said, "Dick, give me a dollar by the end of the day, and you can have this car."

Stammitti did as Patsie asked and ended up with a car.

It was one of many times he came to the aid of someone in need.

Another longtime friend of Patsie's felt his generosity when he was charged with passing a fraudulent check. The man was having health and financial issues at the time. He wrote a bad check at a grocery store for about $300 and the manager called police.

Patsie found out and told his son David to go right away and pay the grocery store $300. David did so, and the man was off the hook.

Still another example is that of Francis Kovach, a former boxer under the name of "Kid Toto" and a dear friend of Patsie's, who always knew he could count on Patsie for generous donations to military veterans' groups in Northeast Ohio.

Kovach frequently dropped in to see Patsie to make a plea for some important needs. He was a decorated World War II veteran who worked tirelessly as a volunteer. Patsie could never say no to "Kid Toto."

The stories and examples demonstrate the depth of Patsie's bigheartedness. Perhaps it was something he developed because he grew up with little, and so, when he earned money, he wanted to share it with others.

"Because of his openhearted and openhanded generosity to so many, I think that we can safely say that Patsie really did know God and God's love because we know that he loved his neighbor," said the Rev. Kenneth Wolnowski in his eulogy for Patsie. "Undoubtedly, Patsie then heard the words that the Master addressed to his servants in the parable of the talents (Matthew 25:14–30). 'Well done. You are an industrious and reliable servant. Come, share your master's joy.'"

AGAINST ALL ODDS / THE PATSIE CAMPANA STORY

It was at the emotional funeral service that the Campana family heard stories of how Patsie significantly helped many people—whose stories were not known before then.

Those whom he helped were from a cross-section of the community: young, old, the needy, the afflicted. He related to them all; he could talk to the guy sweeping the floor, he could talk to the President of the United States. That's just the kind of person he was.

He was a giver, and he gave without expecting anything. As it says in Luke 6:35, "But love your enemies, do good, and lend, expecting nothing in return. Your reward will be great."

SANTINA CAMPANA, A DISTANT COUSIN, IS IN THE PROCESS OF BEATIFICATION

Santina Campana, a third cousin of the Campana family, held a special place in Patsie Campana's heart. While he never met her, she is well-known in the L'Aquila province of Italy for her religious life.

Bobby, Jeneé and Patti attended a celebration marking the birth of Santina Campana in Alfedena, Italy.

A canonization process is underway for Santina, who lived from 1929 to 1950. She is now in the beatification stage, in which religious and other authorities verify if posthumous intervention has performed a miracle.

CHAPTER 9

Patsie's mother, Maria, told her children how Santina visited groups of children, and the sick and elderly, to pray the Rosary. One story told how there was a little boy in an Italian town who had third-degree burns. Santina Campana visited him, put her hand on his feet, and the next day the burns were gone.

Patsie Campana's family had a statue of Santina, and Patsie often put his hand on her statue and said, "You know, boys, we work hard and we're smart, but we're too fortunate. There's something else going on here, and I think she has something to do with it."

Patsie was not an outwardly religious person. But in that aspect, he was: he had faith in how Santina could intervene in his life and the life of others.

Here are some biographical notes on Santina Campana:

She was born on February 2, 1929, in Alfedena (L'Aquila province). Santina was the seventh of nine children of Giuseppe Campana and Margherita Di Palma, peasants in the small mountain town located in the Abruzzo region.

Three sisters and two brothers went into religious orders. But when they moved away, it meant that at an early age, Santina had to help tend the 15 cattle and flock of 150 sheep the family owned.

On June 11, 1936, at the age of 7, she received her First Communion. She wrote in her diary, "Let me die young and make Paradise in white with gowns red."

Numerous episodes were reported by family, friends, and peers about her devotion to Christ, the Madonna, and the Saints, despite her young age.

During World War II, German troops invaded Italy. Santina and her family took refuge in the woods of the mountains, living in abandoned farmhouses through long and cold winters. Santina, nearly 15 years old, became the faith leader of a group of resistance fighters, though she developed a severe case of pleurisy that brought widespread pain and high fever.

On June 26, 1944, Alfedena's inhabitants returned to their ravaged homes, and the Campana family resumed farming.

continued on page 118

AGAINST ALL ODDS / THE PATSIE CAMPANA STORY

continued from page 117

After the war, Santina went to Rome to be admitted as a postulant among the Sisters of Charity. She was admitted to the novitiate, taking on her religious dress with great joy.

But her lung condition had developed into tuberculosis by 1947, and Santina entered a sanitarium in the mountains of Abruzzo. Despite her failing health, she continued to have a cheerful disposition and give encouragement to others.

From her "white throne," as she called her bed, she attracted afflicted souls and comforted them. She asked the doctors not to give her sedation because she wanted to be vigilant and accept pain with joy.

Santina passed away in 1950. Her grave in the town cemetery of Pescina quickly became the destination of pilgrims as the wonders of her intercession grew.

The tomb of Santina Campana is located in the Church of St. Joseph in Pescina, Italy.

On September 3, 1977, her body was interred into the parish church of St. Joseph in Pescina. Each year, the town of Alfedena holds a celebration on Santina's birthday, February 2.

CHAPTER 10

THE SPECIAL FRIENDSHIP

Blessed with a magnetic personality, Patsie developed many friendships during his lifetime. He was a likeable character, charming, witty—and curt when needed. He was an extrovert, and seemingly gained energy from working with other people. This combination made him an excellent match with the person who became one of his best friends, Leo Koury.

Patsie and Leo Koury treasured their longtime friendship. This was taken at Patsie's 60th birthday party.

The two had a bond that began as children on a Lorain school playground. Today, even though Patsie has passed away, the Campana and Koury families remain close. But if it weren't for a bullying incident on that playground, the Campanas and Kourys might not have ever met.

Koury recalls the encounter this way: "I was about 9 or 10 years old. Me and a bunch of kid were hanging out at Harrison Elementary School, about a block away from my home. We were running around, kicking a ball, and a couple teenagers were shooting craps and pitching pennies. Patsie was among them; he was a bit older than me.

"Of course, we younger kids were curious, so we went over to see what was going on," Koury said. "One of the teenagers, an ornery kid who was tall and could be a bit of a bully said, 'Get away, kid!' I said that we were just watching, but he walked over, and hit me in the head with his open palm. Patsie, who was much shorter than the bully, went up to him, popped him in the mouth and pushed him to the ground. The bully got up and fled.

"From that point forward, Patsie became my hero and best friend. The next time Patsie saw the bully trying to pick on me, he walked up to him and said 'Leave that kid alone. Don't you ever touch him again or I'll pound you for it.'"

They remained close friends until Patsie enlisted in the U.S. Navy during World War II. Regrettably, Patsie lost touch with Leo until the 1960s, when they rekindled the relationship.

Patsie and Leo Koury at 28th Street.

"The ironic thing was that he came back to Lorain, Ohio, after traveling all over the world with six kids—five sons and one daughter—and opened an office on West Park Drive," Koury said. "I happened to see the sign that said P.C. Campana, Inc., so I went up to the building, found Patsie, and said, 'My, this is a nice building.' My father's saloon

CHAPTER 10

and building had burned down because of a restaurant fire next door, and I asked Patsie's advice on rebuilding it."

After that, their friendship now reignited, blossomed—as did their combined circle of friends. Patsie even arranged a trip for the Kourys to join him in Spain, where Patsie was going to meet with business associate Egon Evertz.

"They were going to discuss business, and Patsie wanted my wife and I to go with him and his wife," Koury said. "We stayed at the same hotel in Spain. Evertz flew in on his own plane from Germany, and volunteered to fly us from there to Paris."

"But he was drinking, and it was a party atmosphere, so we opted to take another plane. Patsie, his wife, my wife, and I flew to Paris and spent the weekend there. We had a great time."

Soon, Patsie made a point of bumming around with Leo on Saturdays.

"He'd pull up with his big Mercedes-Benz—I used to kid him. I would say, 'You 'Driving Miss Daisy?'—like the movie when the chauffeur drove Miss Daisy all around. I was Miss Daisy. He'd always pick me up and ask, 'Where do you want to go?' I would reply, 'What do you think I am, your social manager?' He'd laugh. He didn't care; he was a very humble guy. And he trusted me so that whatever I wanted, he'd agreed to it."

Leo once wanted to buy the Mercedes-Benz.

Patsie said, "No, I'm not going to sell it to you."

Leo asked why.

"Because I don't want to ruin our friendship," Patsie told him. "I'm going to give it to the dealership, and then you can get it at the dealership if you want, but I'm not going to be a part of selling you my Mercedes."

When Patsie had a private jet for his company, he never used it except for business. Leo once asked, "What kind of friend are you? You've got a jet, and you never take me anywhere."

"One time, when I was in the office, he called and asked, 'What are you doing?' I said, 'I'm trying to make a living. I'm not a big shot like you,' and

121

he said, 'Well, I'll meet you at the airport. I'm going to fly you to Canada.' 'I don't want to go to Canada.' He said, 'I'll show you how to fly.'"

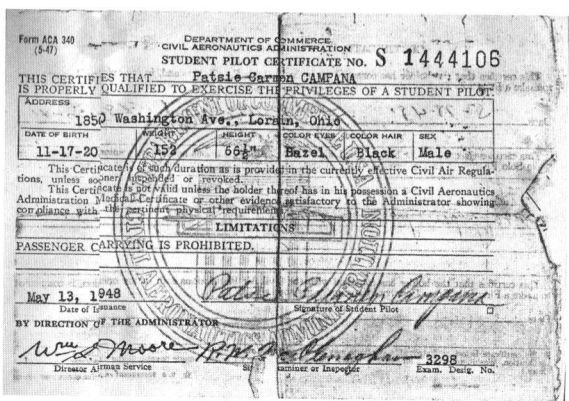

Patsie earned his student pilot license in 1948.

Patsie had learned basic flying skills when he received his student pilot license in 1948. And, he wanted to share them with his friend.

"'OK,' Leo said.

"So, I got there and, sure enough, he turned the controls over to me to fly," Koury recalled. "I just flew it a little bit; I didn't know how."

Sometime after that, Patsie and Leo flew to Atlantic City with their wives.

"That's when we walked in to Caesar's Palace and saw all these photographers and news people around one guy; it was Tommy Lasorda, manager of the Los Angeles Dodgers," Koury said, adding that Lasorda was going to be roasted at a fundraising dinner.

"When I saw him, I said, 'Who are you?' He said, 'Who in the hell are you?' He said it to me after I said that because he's famous, and I was acting like I didn't know who he was. "I'm the Lebanese who let my daughter marry an Italian." He said, 'Lebanese? My godfather's Lebanese.' He always had a comeback.

Patsie just watched his friend bantering back and forth with the baseball legend.

"I think tickets were two for $2,000," Koury recalled. "I told

CHAPTER 10

TIFFANY'S WAS THE PLACE TO BE FOR THE INNER CIRCLE

A local restauranteur named Frank Provenza owned and operated Tiffany's in Elyria. It was there that a network of Patsie's friends would meet for Saturday breakfast in the 1980s and early 1990s.

The restaurant was normally closed that day of the week, but the group met there and cooked up their own specialties. Karel Fiser and Provenza were renowned for their cuisine.

Fiser, Provenza, Dr. Jana Fiserova, Tony LaRizza, and Leo Koury were in the breakfast group. Occasionally, Mike Marsico from P.C. Campana would join them. He recalls the experiences:

> *They would all go there, cook in the kitchen, sit there, and eat and talk. And Frankie Provenza would bring his diamonds and put them out; 'Anybody want to buy a diamond?' I had to go with Patsie every Saturday. But the discussions, the talk; everything was just—it was just so interesting and such a learning experience. And it was like business was out of the question; nobody talked about their normal business. It was all friendship.*
>
> *I used to get a big chuckle out of how Patsie talked about his kids. He was tough on the kids; he really was. But my dad was tough on me, and I knew that was the tradition.*
>
> *I used to tell his kids, 'You know, that's the way your dad is. Just learn to live with it.' But they always had their mother on the sidelines. Even if they lost their job, mom took care of them.*
>
> *Patsie knew that* [and he would never go against Jeneé because her word was law]. *I had a problem with his brother-in-law one time, and I talked to him about it.*
>
> *"'Mike, you know that's my wife's brother,' Patsie said. 'Yeah, I know,' I said and Patsie replied, 'You know what it's like when you go home and your wife's mad at you?' And I told him that I got it.*

Leo Koury remembered one Saturday when Patsie pulled him aside:

> *'Leo, you know I like these guys,'* Patsie said.

continued on page 124

Lasorda, 'I wouldn't pay 25 bucks to cross the street to see you.' He said, 'You smartass, you.'"

"'When you get me a ticket, call me,' and I walked away," Koury said. "Patsie got embarrassed. He said, 'God; you've got a big mouth.' I said, 'I guess that's why I'm a lawyer.'"

But Lasorda came through with some tickets after all. Patsie looked over to Koury's wife, Lila and said, "Boy, I wish I could talk like Leo."

Leo turned to him and said, "I wish I could make money like you can."

"That kind of banter showed our close relationship," reflected Koury.

At Patsie's funeral, Leo delivered a powerful eulogy and moving tribute to his longtime friend. It drew a standing ovation from the mourners—an unusual show of appreciation for a speaker at a funeral.

Leo was the final speaker, following Patsie's business associates Dick Colella and Al Hillegass. Here is his eulogy:

This will probably be the toughest speech I ever give. That's something for a lawyer to say, but it is a eulogy of my best friend.

---

continued from page 123

Except—he liked them as friends, and that was the common part of Patsie. But he said to me, "Leo, you know I like those guys like you do, but you and I are special." I about fainted. He was afraid that the others were going to curry favor with me more than with him. And I'm common as they come. There's nothing sophisticated about me. I'll never forget that time he told me that.

Tiffany's closed in 1992, but Provenza wasn't done in the restaurant business. In 1996, he opened Pasquale's Pasta House, an Italian restaurant in Elyria, with his partner Karel Fiser. It was named after not only Provenza's father, but after Patsie (whose real first name was Pasquale) as well. It was sold in 2003.

CHAPTER 10

I am fortunate that I can say that I had a best friend. Not many people can say that in their lifetime. The dictionary defines a friend as a person who likes another, a companion, a comrade, a chum. My definition of P.C. was to know all of his faults and still love him, and he the same of me.

I had the privilege of knowing him since my childhood. However, our paths went in different directions for several years, he into the Navy and throughout the world in steel mills. What people don't know about him was his courage in the Navy as a deep-sea diver. He would never tell you, but I found out from family and friends, how he landed at Iwo Jima and volunteered to retrieve, under fire, the bodies of our servicemen and bring them back so they could be buried. As you know, Iwo Jima was one of our biggest losses in our campaign during World War II. He also dove at Tokyo Bay to clear up landmines and other things.

P.C. was truly one of a kind. A very unique human being. In fact, he had more humanity and love for his family and friends and strangers in need than any man I knew. As you all know, he was born in Abruzzo, Italy, in the Apennine Mountains, and came to America as an infant. He was often proud of his heritage and he used to say to me, a man who denies his heritage has none; he is without culture or family.

He gave the appearance of a common, ordinary working man. He had an explosive temper when he felt a person was not true or fair to anyone. But his intemperance was short-lived and forgiving. His greatest quality was that he had character: his honesty, his industry, his loyalty, and his courage. Patsie was a very humble and generous man. He was a true philanthropist, always helping churches, schools, hospitals, organizations, and many needy people. Right now, he would be embarrassed and would want to clip me for even talking about it.

He personified the American dream, a first-generation American of immigrant parents who was self-educated by hard work and on-the-job training, always relating to when he was a welder at the American shipyard, then an electrician, then a foreman and then a superintendent; never faltering or goofing off, but always learning. A man of that background becoming a giant in the steel industry is the most remarkable achievement that this community will ever see.

The remarkable thing about him was that, at the age of 48, having six children, he left the security of his job as the head of a company and started on his own from scratch to build this empire that you see today. Truly the captain of industry.

He was the most caring and concerned person about his siblings, Baldo, Albert, and Rosemary, and their families' needs, always talking to me about them, grateful to Rosemary for taking care of mom so he could get the things accomplished to take care of the rest of the family. He loved his wife, Jenee, his daughter, Patti Ann, his sons David, Larry, Bobby, Scotti, Corky, and all his grandchildren more than life itself. He was a big pussycat. He didn't want anybody to know it.

I offer a challenge today to all the family and friends, in the words of President John F. Kennedy on this 30th anniversary of his death from his inaugural address that should apply to all of you. We dare not forget today that you are the heirs of P.C. Campana. Let the word go forth from this time and place, to friends and foe alike,

CHAPTER 10

that the torch has been passed to a new generation of Campanas, born in this century, tempered by hard work, disciplined by a taskmaster father, proud of his Italian heritage and unwilling to witness or permit the deterioration of all his hard work and success. Let every person know, whether a fellow worker or a competitor, whether they wish you well or ill, that you are the heirs, will pay any price, bear any burden, meet any hardship, support any friends, oppose any foe to ensure the survival of the P.C. Campana group and its continued success. One for all and all for one is the pledge to the memory of your father.

And to you, friends, Saturdays will never be the same at Tiffany's Restaurant for Frank Provenza, Karel Fiser, Tony LaRizza, Dr. Jana Fiserova, and myself. However, I would also like to acknowledge one of his dearest friends who honors the Campana family to appear here, Attorney General Lee Fisher, who is one of the few public officials that Patsie could stand. Patsie would point a finger at him and lecture him and talk to him like he was talking to a member of the family. And the brilliant Lee Fisher would sit there and listen. Whether he was listening or not we never knew, but at least he gave him the appearance. Thank you, Lee.

And to the friends, I offer a passage from the Rubaiyat of Omar Khayyam, as you know, from my side of the Mediterranean.

> *'The Moving Finger writes; and, having writ,*
> *Moves on: nor all thy Piety nor Wit*
> *Shall lure it back to cancel half a Line,*
> *Nor all thy Tears wash out a Word of it.'*

And the last thing I could say is what was said to me when my father died after a brief career and life and died at the age of 47, I buried him on my 23rd birthday, there is nothing else we can say at this time except to go forth, family and friends, and be the person he would have wanted you to be so that they look at you and say, 'There are Patsie's children, there is Patsie's friend and his name carries on.' He will live in my heart till the day I die. God rest his soul.

CHAPTER 11

NOVEMBER 24, 1993: THE DAY PATSIE WAS CALLED HOME

Patsie Campana lived life to the fullest. Even as he entered his 70s, he kept an active schedule. However, he quietly had reached a point in his life where he was not just thinking about today… but what tomorrow might look like without him.

In the late spring/early summer of 1993, John Zalick sat in Patsie's office as the two men reviewed company financial reports. Patsie suddenly looked up at John and said, "If I'm not around, you've got to give me your word you will help take care of my family and help them with this business."

As Zalick recalled, "It was just an out-of-the-blue kind of thing where we were talking about something else, then he suddenly brought this up. And with him just being in his early 70s, that was unusual. I knew he had had some episodes with his health, so he was doing some logical thinking to plan ahead. I gave my word that I would and we shook hands. He then thanked me."

By the late 1980s Patsie had, indeed, made plans. He knew his company had grown to the point where it was no longer one big entity and wanted to make sure it did not face singular corporate exposure. He recognized that different product lines had higher liability risks than others, and had the foresight to discuss this with his advisors. Patsie's moves ensured any future problem would be contained to the one company as opposed to the entire entity. The family's financial health was very important, and Patsie made sure to protect it. After meeting with his advisors, The Campana Group was reorganized into a multiple entity structure.

Around the same time, Patsie called his son Scotti, and asked him to meet at the Campana Café for lunch.

Patsie's sister, Rosemary, was running it, and made Scotti a cheeseburger while Patsie had a beer.

During the meal, Patsie told Scotti he thought he was going to die. He said hadn't been taking his heart medicine and gave his son a napkin on which he had written seven things to do.

Scotti promised to get the things done.

A couple of those items involved helping Rosemary, as well as completing some tasks around the Campana home. But the last item was to find a man named Freddie Barreiro and help him build a boxing gym in Lorain.

Scotti didn't know Freddie Barreiro, but soon learned about him.

A two-time Golden Gloves champ in Puerto Rico who came to the United States in the 1950s, Barreiro started a boxing program for the neighborhood kids. By 1998, a few years after Patsie's death, the gym was built. Scotti kept his promise to his father.

Today, it is still in operation as Freddie's Boxing Club and offers a boxing program for about 60 boys.

While Patsie didn't talk to others about his health problems, some co-workers saw his health beginning to deteriorate.

Karen Trautwein recalls how Patsie looked the last time she saw him: "He was sitting at his desk, rubbing his arm, and looked a little pale to me," she said. "But he said he was fine."

It was November, and Patsie was scheduled to travel to Pennsylvania the following day with his brother Baldo to view a Babcock & Wilcox steel mill that was for sale.

He got up and walked toward the door.

As Karen recalls, she said, "I know you're going to get upset, but you don't look well—something's wrong."

CHAPTER 11

Patsie shook her off. "I'm fine," he said. "I'm going home. I'm going tomorrow, and I'll see you in two days."

And then, he walked out the door.

The next day, Patsie and Baldo went to look at the steel mill. He returned home afterward, took a shower, and found that he couldn't stop sweating.

Jeneé thought he looked pale and said, "There's something wrong, Patsie."

Finally, that evening, Patsie was taken to the emergency room by Larry, Bobby and Jeneé. He was admitted to St. Joseph's Hospital Tuesday, November 23, 1993. His tests revealed that he suffered a heart attack, but he was stable and was assigned a room for further testing and observation.

Early Wednesday morning, the hospital called Bobby about Patsie's worsening condition. Bobby contacted the family and everyone immediately rushed to St. Joseph's Hospital as Patsie was suffering another heart attack, but complained of only minor discomfort.

Patsie's brothers Baldo and Albert and sister Rosemary were called in. Friends Leo Koury, Dick Colella and Mike Marsico came as well. All were there to comfort each other during this most stressful time.

When Patsie spoke with Koury, he said, "I think this is it." Koury said, "No, you'll be all right." Patsie said, "I love you," and Koury answered, "I love you more."

"That was hard for him to say," Koury remembered. "He wanted to say that. Nobody was closer to me than him as a friend."

Things took a turn for the worse. Doctors tried to stabilize Patsie in hopes of having him transferred to Elyria Memorial Hospital and have a cardiac catheterization procedure.

Even at the hospital, with his family at his bedside, Patsie was conducting business.

"You should've seen the steel mill I saw today," Patsie told the gathered family members. "We're going to buy that son of a bitch."

Patsie also expressed worry about the swimming pool his son Pat Jr. was building. He went over with him, step-by-step, how to secure a superb ground for the electrical system, like one that is used in steel mills.

"I don't want my grandkids getting electrocuted," he demanded—almost as if he would not leave this world until he knew the pool building was safe.

Pat Jr. assured his father that he followed the proper steps, and Patsie relaxed a bit.

But then, after Patsie was stabilized for a short time, he had yet another heart attack. Dr. Francisco Floro, the Campana family physician and dear family friend, worked along with other doctors to save Patsie but after exhaustive efforts, Patsie passed away.

"He was strong," office administrator Karen Trautwein remembers thinking. "When they told me he had a heart attack, I said 'Oh, he'll be fine.'"

Then, when Patsie died a few hours later, she thought, "My God. He seemed indestructible."

Mike Marsico said, "But he went the way I'd like to go. There wasn't much suffering."

It was November 24, 1993, the Wednesday before Thanksgiving. In a way, it was fitting that a man who valued gratitude so much left the earthly world unfinished and moved on to watch over his family from above so they could carry on his philanthropy and legacy.

At the Reidy-Scanlan Funeral Home in Lorain, mourners waited in line for up to two hours to pay their respects. The funeral was held the following Saturday at St. Peter's Church.

Rev. Kenneth J. Wolnowski delivered the Mass. He gave words of comfort to the family and talked of Patsie's life:

> Some wonderful things have been said about Patsie in the news media, and condolences have been coming from near and far. And I am sure you're proud of the tribute by Mayor Alex Olejko, who said that Patsie was the No. 1 citizen of Lorain and is flying the flag at half-

CHAPTER 11

staff over City Hall to grieve his loss. I would like to add the condolences of your parish family, of St. Peter's, our school, and, of course, my own personal condolences.

We share with you the shock of his loss. Just this past Sunday, he was here to celebrate the baptism of his newest granddaughter, Talia Jeneé, Scotti and Kristine's baby girl. He looked robust and healthy, and afterward he was joking around with us as he was surrounded by his grandchildren. I think he said there were 15 of them and many of them usually spent Sundays afternoons at his home. I want to assure you, also, of our prayers; prayers on behalf of his soul, that he may now rest in God's eternal peace and love and also prayers on your behalf as you deal with his loss.

Jesus' parable of the talents can be used, I feel, fittingly as a summary of Patsie's life. Matthew 25:14-30 tells us:

A man entrusted his servants to take care of his property while he was away. To one servants, he gave five talents, to another, two; to another one. The one who had received the five talents went off at once and traded with them, and made five more talents. In the same way, the one who had the two talents made two more talents. But the one who had received the one talent went off and dug a hole in the ground and hid his master's money. After a long time, the master of those servants came and settled accounts with them. Then the one who had received the five talents came forward, bringing five more talents, saying, "Master, you handed over to me five talents; see, I have made five more talents." His master said to him, 'Well done. You are an industrious and reliable servant. Come, share your master's joy.'

And the one with the two talents also came forward, saying, 'Master, you handed over to me two talents; see, I have made two more talents.' His master said to him, 'Well done. You are an industrious and reliable servant. Come, share your master's joy.'

Then the one who had received the one talent also came forward, saying, 'Master, I knew that you were a harsh man, reaping where you did not sow, and gathering where you did not scatter seed; so I was afraid, and I went and hid your talent in the ground. Here you have what is yours." But his master replied, 'You wicked and lazy slave! You knew, did you, that I reap where I did not sow, and gather where I did not scatter? Then you ought to have invested my money with the bankers, and on my return, I would have received what was my own with interest.'

'So, take the talent from him, and give it to the one with the 10 talents. For to all those who have, more will be given, and they will have an abundance; but from those who have nothing, even what they have will be taken away. As for this worthless servant, throw him into the outer darkness, where there will be weeping and gnashing of teeth.'

Patsie came into this world on November 17, 1920, in Barrea, Italy, of humble beginnings. Then and there, God the Master entrusted unto him, as in the parable the master entrusted them unto the servants, God entrusted to Patsie his specialness—his individuality, his personality, his talents and abilities; his almost unlimited potential. And we all know the story well of what Patsie did with that potential. He came to this country, he developed his knowledge, his experience, his skills as an engineer, as a businessman, an administrator, rising through the ranks until finally he formed his own P.C. Campana, serving as the chairman of the board and the chief executive officer.

First and foremost, however, Patsie was a family man. And I know his children well. I can see that his spirit

CHAPTER 11

is really reflected in the close and loving relationship that exists between his children, his daughter and son-in-law, the grandchildren and of course always, always with the greatest reverence and respect and honor and love to Jeneé.

And so, like the servants in the parable, he doubled the talents that were entrusted to him. But what he did with those talents is even more important. And so, he courageously and honorably served his country as a frogman in the Pacific during the Second World War, and then of course there is the lengthy, lengthy and detailed story of Patsie Campana the philanthropist. Examples of his philanthropy were reported in newspaper articles recently. I know personally that there was an almost constant stream of requests for help from Patsie from every manner of worthy cause, each day. And he responded as best he could. As pastor of St. Peter's Church parish, I was hesitant to approach him also for help, knowing all the demands that are made upon him every day but whenever we did ask for something as a parish, he always was more than generous in responding. Many times, we didn't even ask. He just took the initiative and offered his gifts and his generous support.

He was also personally generous to me. Just one example that I can think of—when I sat with him at Scotti and Kristine's wedding rehearsal dinner at Tiffany's, his favorite restaurant, he said he wanted to order me a special entrée, if that would be all right. I said of course. He called over Frank Provenza, the owner of the restaurant, and he told Frank to prepare me a Steak Diane dinner. When it came, he was very anxious to see what I thought of it, whether I liked it. Well, of course I loved it. The next day Mrs. Campana came to the rectory with a gift from herself and Patsie, an entire beef tenderloin, not the kind you could buy in any grocery store, so that we could cut it up and make filets and have all the steak Diane we would ever want.

In the second reading of sacred Scripture this morning, we heard, 'Let us love one another, for love comes from God.' It also says whoever loves God must also love his neighbor. Because of all his openhearted and openhanded generosity to so many, I think that we can safely say that Patsie really did know God, and God's love because we know that he loved his neighbor. Undoubtedly, Patsie then heard the words that the master addressed to his servants in this morning's parable: 'Well done. You are an industrious and reliable servant. Come, share your master's joy.'

And so today we give God our thanks for the gift of Patsie Campana, for the years that he lived, and for the joys and sorrows, the good times and the bad, the ups and downs, that made his life unique and unrepeatable. And we thank God for our faith, which convinces us that God who endowed Patsie with a gift of life on this earth has not taken that gift away. So Patsie then lives in our hearts, he lives in our memories, he lives in the legacy that he leaves behind for his family to continue, but most important of all, he lives with God, reunited with his parents, and his brother Lawrence Dino killed in World War II. We all look forward to the day when we all will be reunited on the other side of physical death where in the words of Psalm 30, 'Our mourning will be turned into dancing. We will be clothed with joy. We will sing psalms to God unceasingly, and we will thank our God forever.'

Patsie's longtime business partner, Al Hillegass, spoke next:

First, I would like to express my sympathy and great grief on this occasion. I would also like to thank today

CHAPTER 11

Jeneé and the Campana family for asking me to participate in this service. The words I say, which will be few, I say as a representative of our companies, our Camp-Hill companies, and all our Camp-Hill associates who were just as saddened as you are.

He was my business partner; no man could have a greater partner. Believe me, no man could have a greater partner. To know Patsie was a privilege. To be his friend and partner was a great honor, and I shall cherish that for the rest of my life. He labored in the same vineyards as I did, the steel business, 50 years in that business; a hard, rough business. Never did I meet a more enthusiastic, innovative and energetic person than P.C. Of all the people I have met in the industry, nobody could hold a candle to all those qualities that I have just mentioned for this man.

Failure was not in his vocabulary. I would tell him we have a problem, and he would say we don't have problems, Al, we have opportunities. When I said it looks like we were going to fail at this thing, he would say, 'No, no, we're just not succeeding at the rate we figured we would, but we will succeed.'

So to my good friend, I bid farewell. I wish him well. His work on this earth is finished. We can say, 'Rest in peace, well done, thy good and faithful servant. You are gone, but your memory will linger on forever.' Thank you.

Dick Collela, Patsie's long-time attorney, followed:

Patsie Campana came to us from a small village in Italy, next to a crystal clear blue lake, nestled in the Apennine Mountains, only a few kilometers from the birthplace of my own parents. Patsie was possessed of

> *a pioneering spirit, boundless energy and a passionate desire to succeed in everything that he did. And succeed he did. He is the personification of the American dream, an inspiration to all of us.*
>
> *Patsie accomplished all that he set out to do, but to Patsie his greatest accomplishment and achievement was his family, his wife Jeneé, their six children, their 15 grandchildren. It was the love of his family that motivated Patsie, and it is this family that will carry on his dreams and goals from generation to generation.*
>
> *While most will remember Patsie as a pre-eminently successful businessman, industrialist and philanthropist, those of us who knew him in a special way will remember him as a friend with a twinkle in his eye from that small village next to the lake nestled in the mountains. God bless you, Patsie.*

Colella's words were followed by a nearly 15-minute eulogy by Patsie's best friend, Leo Koury, after which the attendees gave a standing ovation, a rarity at a funeral service. The powerful tribute was presented earlier in this book, but the charge he gave deserves repeating:

> *Let the word go forth from this time and place to friends and foe alike that the torch has been passed to a new generation of Campanas, born in this century, tempered by hard work, disciplined by a taskmaster father, proud of his Italian heritage and unwilling to witness or permit the deterioration of all his hard work and success.*

When it came time to place a tombstone at Calvary Cemetery for Patsie, Jeneé wanted to add the slogan, "I Did It My Way" (the title of a popular Frank Sinatra song) to the stone—but it would break the rules for the standardized style at the cemetery.

CHAPTER 11

Patsie's epitaph: "I Did It My Way."

However, in true Patsie Campana-style, the family found a way to have the phrase added to the stone, and under the cloak of darkness, had the stone installed at the gravesite.

Many have said that "I did it my way" sums up Patsie's legacy—he wanted to live life to the fullest and do it the only way he knew how. He loved his family, and made sure he took care of everything the right way. But Patsie always had to do it his way… and that meant doing whatever was necessary to succeed against all odds.

Easter 1988

PART FOUR

THE NEXT GENERATION

CHAPTER 12

THE TORCH IS PASSED TO OTHERS IN THE CAMPANA FAMILY

Shortly after Patsie's death, Bobby Campana and his brother Pat Jr. were attending an event at Elyria Country Club. In the men's room, two men were talking about the Campanas, not realizing they were within earshot range of Pat Jr.

"You see the Campana kids are here tonight?" one asked the other. "Well, they won't be here long. The old man's gone now; that thing's going down the tubes."

When Pat relayed the conversation to Bobby, he mentioned how much it upset him. The two men discussed their mutual concerns—something they hadn't really talked about since their father's death. But it was the proverbial elephant in the room. They had seen other companies break up or fail after the founder died, and together wondered if the same thing happen could happen to P.C. Campana.

The two came to an agreement: Even though many observers may have been waiting for the company to fail, there was absolutely no way they would allow this to happen. This rallying cry became a shared commitment among all the Campana children and family members. They agreed it would be a sin for the company to "go down the tubes" after all the hard work Patsie had put into it. And so, they set to work.

One of the first matters that needed to be addressed was company ownership. Patsie's hard work led to one of the largest estates ever filed in Lorain County Probate Court. Terms of Patsie's will transferred ownership to Jeneé. But she had no intention of running the company, so the family got together and developed a plan of action to move forward.

The Campana family, Easter 1988.

It was determined that Jeneé and Patti would handle administrative duties. Larry would focus on sales. Pat Jr. would guide the operation, Bobby would run the financial department, and Scotti worked in sales.

David was not involved in the company; he had been fired by Patsie six months before he died and was working for another business.

This arrangement was not exactly an ideal solution, and it soon became obvious that there were too many chiefs involved. Jeneé recognized she needed some legal advice, so the family turned to Patsie's longtime friend, Leo Koury, for help.

"Jenee called me and said, 'Leo, I'd like to hire you,'" Koury said. "I said, 'Hire me? For what?' I would never charge them or get involved. 'What's the problem?'"

"Leo, you gave a speech at the wake on what John F. Kennedy said about the torch being passed, about staying together while there are forces trying to pull us apart," Jeneé said. "I want you to represent me, bring the children all into the conference room at the Campana office, and explain to them what they should do."

Koury said, "I told her, 'OK. I want a retainer: $1. She said, 'What?' I said, '$1.' I asked for a retainer of $1 to let them know that I was not there to make money—not acting like a lawyer, but I would advise them as a friend, and I would let them know it's serious."

CHAPTER 12

Leo did as Jeneé asked and met with the family.

When Leo spoke with the family, it was as if the words were straight from Patsie. It captivated the Campanas.

"I told them, 'Look; do you see your hand? Each finger is important," Koury said. "Each child is important. One of you may succeed while the others fail, but that doesn't make that hand strong; it means it starts to deteriorate."

"Then I told them, 'My pledge to you and my pledge to your father was that you stick together, because he gave you all the greatest opportunity to perpetuate his name; everything he did was for all of you. If you're doing something else than that, you're dishonoring his name—you will not be perpetuating his name, and he deserves that."

The Campana family heeded Leo's sage words of advice and restructured the way the company was run. Today, David is president and CEO. Mike Marsico is its COO. David watches the numbers, gives the COO direction, and ensures he executes his duties. Mike is held accountable for his actions and no one can go behind his back.

David computerized the company. He implemented software that established an audit trail, holding everyone accountable for what they do. This network was installed in 1995, at a time when networks were in their infancy. The company therefore became an early adopter, ensuring it had the most up-to-date technology tools, including e-mail and Internet access, to remain competitive.

As the company benefitted from more efficient operations, it soon became time to review the role of the next generation's involvement in the family business.

At that time, there were 15 grandchildren. So, the question became: Should they learn the ropes and eventually become owners?

Patsie's daughter, Patti, expressed concern that the grandchildren would be either treated with resentment or spoiled by lax management when they began working for the company.

There were already some instances of that.

Further, rivalries and other issues might arise. Some family businesses have seen less passion in successive generations and less work ethic than what was optimum. The Campana children had invested their lives in growing the company; the grandchildren, although talented and competent, didn't have to build a company from the ground up, so they didn't have the same innate relationship with it.

As a result, Patti pushed for a policy to prohibit the grandchildren from working for the company.

When it came up for a vote, all the Campana siblings approved the motion.

Today, the only grandchild who works for the company is Kristian Campana, David's eldest son. Kristian was employed before the new rule went into effect, and therefore his position was grandfathered in.

Once the new management was in place, a restructuring process began.

Patsie had been reluctant to give up control of his company, so there was no written succession plan in place. Jeneé, who inherited the business, was more than willing to spread the ownership equally among the six children. After some legal work was completed, each child was subsequently made an equal owner of the corporation.

Currently, in addition to P.C. Campana, the family also operates a family office for investments. The focus is a diversification portfolio through real estate, private equity, and venture capital. Together, they enjoy numerous long-term investment relationships across the country. If Patsie were alive today, he would be very proud of his children and how they took his legacy and expanded it beyond the company's walls.

CHAPTER 13

THE CAMPANA FAMILY DIVERSIFIES

During Patsie's life, purchasing real estate for expansion was nothing new for him and his family. So back in 1984, he had incorporated West Park Limited, Inc. to become P.C. Campana's real estate arm. Bob Campana was named West Park president, and all real estate purchases from that point forward went through West Park. Accordingly, after Patsie's death, as part of the family's diversification strategy, developing real estate became the next logical step for the family.

It began in earnest less than a year after Patsie's death. On July 25, 1995, the company broke ground on a 31-acre P.C. Campana Industrial Park. The park offered a new concept, spec building, in which light industrial spaces were created in speculation of future tenants. The buildings were designed with flexible uses in mind, giving options for possible tenants.

Not stopping there, West Park Limited then proposed a 162-cluster-home development near Jaeger Road in Lorain. The resulting Camden Ridge Development was announced in 1999. Homes started selling in 2003 on streets with familiar family names such as Jeneé Drive (after Patsie's wife) and Santina Way (after Santina Campana, Patsie's cousin who is being considered for sainthood).

West Park Limited currently holds a significant portfolio of investment outside of real estate, including, but not limited to, angel investments, private equity and venture capital investments, and numerous fund investments across the country.

Beyond real estate, because Patsie was so involved in charitable giving, the family wanted to continue those efforts as well. In 1995, they established The Campana Foundation. Its focus became to inspire others to find hope in the Campanas' story of humble beginnings and to achieve the American Dream by believing in themselves, working hard, declaring vision, and hungering for education.

One recipient of a Campana Foundation grant was the Elyria-based youth outreach organization, Save Our Children. The group's mission is to improve literacy, cultivate leadership skills through mentoring, and promote academic excellence among the at-risk youth. Save Our Children operates an after-school and summer program for children in first through eighth grade, as well as a teen mentoring program for high school students.

Other recipients over the years have included the Community Health Partners Foundation, the Lorain Palace Civic Center, the former Lorain Catholic High School, St. Ignatius High School in Cleveland, St. Peter Church in Lorain, Genesis House domestic violence shelter, Junior Achievement of Greater Lorain County, the Lorain County Free Clinic, the Blessing House children's crisis care center in Lorain, the Italian American Veterans Post of Lorain, the Village Project in Bay Village, the Achievement Centers for Children, TrueNorth Cultural Arts, and the Cleveland State University Foundation.

In addition, the Alfred J. Loser, M.D. Memorial Scholarship Fund, overseen by Patsie's best friend, Leo Koury, established the Patsie Campana Award in Patsie's honor. The scholarship is given to a student of exceptional achievement, regardless of race, creed, or color, who is a Lorain High School graduate and who is in need and worthy.

The most visible manifestation of Patsie's legacy stands on the campus of Lorain County Community College: the Patsie C. Campana, Sr. Engineering & Development Center, with its newly added Patsie C. and Dolores Jeneé Campana Center for Ideation and Invention.

CHAPTER 13

A plaque honoring The Patsie and Jeneé Campana Foundation.

At first thought, this may seem an anomaly because Patsie never went to college. But, he made a success of himself that equaled or even surpassed those with college degrees. As those who knew him recognized, Patsie's unquenchable thirst for knowledge was matched only by his desire to inspire others and give back to the community

In 2001, Lorain County Community College named a $6 million facility in his honor to recognize his importance in manufacturing. He would have been pleased—not only was it an institution in Lorain, his home, but it was where new industrial technologies could be utilized by young, talented minds.

The Patsie C. Campana Sr. Engineering and Development Center houses the latest in computer programs and state-of-the-art equipment for students to develop their ideas. It also offers space for start-up companies to get off the ground.

149

The Patsie C. and Dolores Jeneé Campana Center for Ideation and Invention.

In coordination with the center, courses of study are offered that lead to associate degrees in several fields. It has become a place where students can be inspired to follow their dream.

The site, location, and materials used for the building reflect progressive thinking during the project's design phase. They also demonstrate the implementation of innovative construction technologies—echoing how Patsie designed buildings to be practical and sensible.

Located adjacent to the Nord Advanced Technologies Center by design (so existing and new programs could expand and share space during their growth and development), the facility is also located next to the Great Lakes Technology Park—creating a true innovation campus.

The building was underwritten through federal, state, and private (such as from the Campana family) funds.

The Patsie Campana Engineering Center at Lorain County Community College.

CHAPTER 13

Jeneé and Patsie at their son Scotti's wedding in 1990.

As enrollment increased and more programs were needed, a $5 million addition was built: The Patsie C. and Dolores Jeneé Campana Center for Ideation and Invention. This center was also built with a combination of public funds and private donations.

The first phase of the project, a 10,000-square-foot addition, opened in 2017, and features state-of-the-art digital manufacturing labs equipped with high-tech equipment for fabrication, automation, rapid prototyping, and more.

Among the equipment is a modular digital prototyping line with a CNC vertical machining center, a FANUC laser cutter to cut metal, and an OMAX waterjet cutter to cut stone. There are also labs for automation, programmable logic controllers, and robotic welding.

The second phase of the Ideation and Invention Center will be a renovation of the existing Campana Center to create areas that support ideation, including flexible collaboration spaces, project pods, and virtual reality labs where teams can review designs in 3D hologram format.

PART FOUR

Another benefit of the Ideation Center will be to supplement the existing Fab Lab, adding more space for the community to use laser cutters, 3D printers, and other equipment.

The entire innovation ecosystem the Campana Center offers mirrors how Patsie built his success. In one location, it combines the needs of students, industry, and the community and allows innovators to evolve into entrepreneurs—following a path taken by Patsie in his luminous career. And now, future generations of burgeoning entrepreneurs can also reach for their dreams and begin their own journey to overcome the odds.

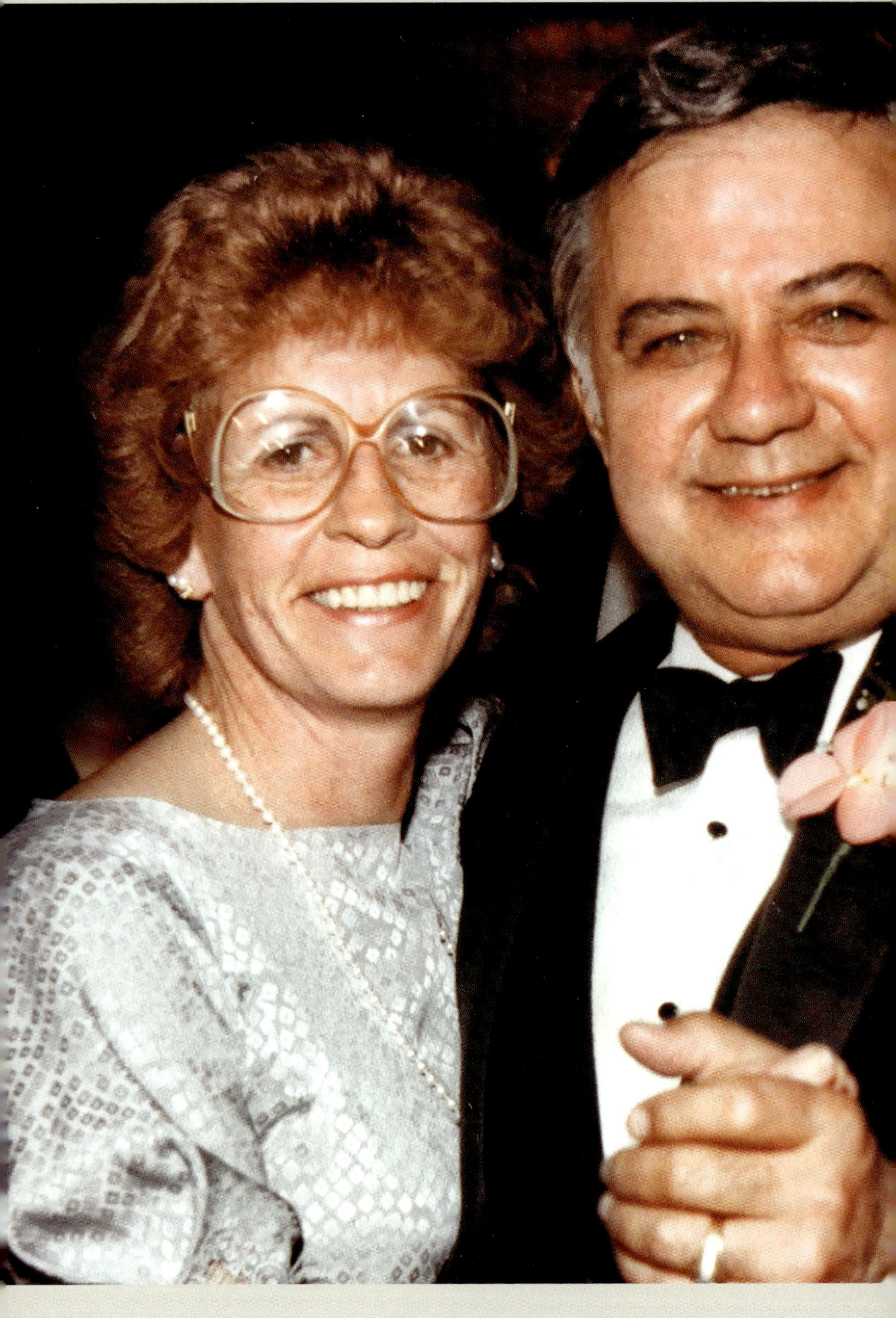

PART FIVE

REFLECTIONS & ANECDOTES
BY LOVED ONES AND FRIENDS

CHAPTER 14

STORIES ABOUT THE MAN UNDERSCORE HIS LIFE... AND LEGEND

John Zalick: First impressions are powerful
In 1985, P.C. Campana was in growing mode and was looking to hire a larger accounting/advising firm that was better qualified than their current firm. John Zalick, a partner at a large local firm (now RSMUS, LLP), which was one of the top contenders for the job. Zalick remembers when he met Patsie on his initial visit to the Campana plant—before RSM had landed the P.C. Campana account.

The first thing Patsie did was demonstrate the Caldo Torch.

When Zalick arrived at the plant, Patsie was nowhere in sight. Zalick and Patsie's son Bobby put on hard hats and went into the plant to find him.

As Zalick explains, when they walked into the factory, standing there was a man in a welder's outfit wielding a torch (who turned out to be Mr. Campana), and a younger guy who was watching him.

Bobby said, "Well, that's my dad. Let me interrupt him."

"So, he interrupts him, and Patsie takes off the safety equipment and we talk in this sort of [out of the way] side office of the plant. I said, 'I saw you out there. What were you doing?' He said, 'Well, I was teaching somebody—this young fellow—how to properly weld,'" Zalick recalled.

"Here's the president—in the plant, where he loved to be the most (which was really telling something about him)—helping this young man learn and giving him on-the-job training."

Then Zalick asked Patsie about his accomplishments.

"Let me show you something," Patsie said. "We have this torch, it's called a Caldo Torch. This thing will cut through anything."

In the scrap yard was a thick steel door, like that of a safe. Patsie lit the torch and cut through the door like it was butter.

He beamed with pride. It was an example of how pleased he was of his products and what they could do.

While the Caldo Torch impressed Zalick, he was also awed by Patsie's personality as they toured the Campana plant.

"Let me take you on a tour to show you what we do and how we operate, what we do for the steel industry, etc.," he told Zalick.

"We just walked around for about two hours, and for him to devote the time, that tells me he was very proud of what he did—and what his people did. Everyone, and I mean everyone, called him Patsie, not 'Mr. Campana.'"

As they walked around the plant, Patsie would stop, shake hands with people, and ask them how they're doing.

"That's the kind of guy he was," Zalick recalled. "He started as a blue-collar worker, and so he never forgot who he was and what his background was. The tour took so long because he stopped and talked. He asked me about my background, as did Bobby, and I could see he was a big guy on relationships with people.

"I think all the while he was making an assessment, he was looking for somebody he could have a business relationship and friendship with. That was key to him, because if he didn't have both with you, you probably weren't going to be around too long, as an employee, an adviser, or anything like that. Then eventually we said goodbye. The next day Bobby called and said 'you're hired.'"

One other story Zalick recalls involves Patsie's trust in people, especially a family member.

"We were talking about financial matters, and he said, 'John, let me tell you something. You know Jeneé works here. Do you know why she works here?' I said, 'Not really. I mean, she's your wife.' He said, 'You always want a trusted family member watching the cash register.' That was pure Patsie—what he believed about his family."

RSM has been the accounting firm for P.C. Campana ever since. In the early 1980s, it helped restructure the company to protect product lines and ensure that the family's assets were protected.

John Zalick: Patsie's generosity even extended to his Sabreliner jet

Zalick's ex-wife and their daughter moved to Hilton Head, South Carolina. Patsie, knowing this, asked if he visited his daughter. Zalick said he flew there periodically to see her.

A company jet meant Patsie spared no expense.

"So Patsie said, 'Oh, OK.' Soon he called back and asked, 'When do you want to go to Hilton Head?' I said, 'Well, my plane leaves at—' and he cut me off. 'I'll just have our plane take you—no cost to you.'"

"Bobby Campana and some others went too, and they played golf while I visited my daughter. Twice I flew on that plane, landed in Hilton Head, saw my daughter, stayed there, and then the plane went on to somewhere else. But for him to even think to ask me and then do something like that was incredible. That was his character. He was concerned about me. I wasn't a family member, but he was concerned about my relationship with my daughter."

Karen Trautwein: What did I get myself into?

When Karen Trautwein had just started with the P.C. Campana in accounts payable, she came back from lunch one day and heard a God-awful noise upstairs.

As she climbed the stairs to investigate, a young man flew by her. Next came Patsie. He came to a full stop, looked at Trautwein, smiled, and said, "Good afternoon!" and then he continued chasing the man out the door.

"It was an ex-employee that was giving us some trouble," Trautwein said. "But I couldn't believe Patsie stopped in the middle of the chase, looked at me, smiled, and said, "Good afternoon," and then started running again. I was thinking, 'Oh my God, what did I get myself into here?'"

Doug Nolfi: Who was that man?

Doug Nolfi, who worked his way up at Camp-Hill Corporation from the maintenance department to president remembers meeting Patsie for the first time—and not knowing it was Patsie.

Nolfi, a veteran of 20 years with Camp-Hill, had been working a few months with the company as a maintenance supervisor. He stopped by the electrical work bench.

"There was a gentleman sitting there talking to one of the electricians. Not knowing who the person was, I asked if there was something that I could help him with (wondering why he was there) and he said, 'No, I am fine; just getting caught up on what is going on.'"

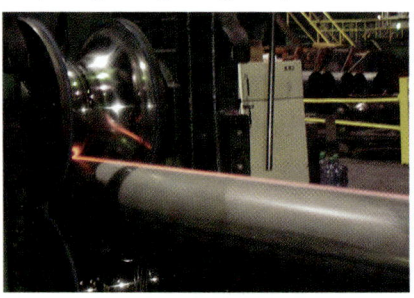

Pipe in production at Camp-Hill

CHAPTER 14

Nolfi walked away a little bewildered. A few moments later, one of the other maintenance personnel asked if he had met Patsie Campana, who was visiting the electricians.

Immediately, Nolfi went back to the electrical desk and introduced himself to Patsie. The two men hit it off, and Patsie encouraged Nolfi to develop a good maintenance crew because it was important to a good mill operation.

In contrast, Nolfi's first meeting with Camp-Hill partner Al Hillegass was a bit different—but the advice was much the same.

"Right after I started, Al Hillegass asked me to stop at his office (which later became my office) and told me that as long as I worked hard, that was all that could be asked of me," Nolfi recalled.

Nolfi continued with Camp-Hill, until U.S. Steel took over the operation and let him go.

"I was fortunate to have the opportunity to work with Bob Campana, who had a lot of the same qualities that his father did in respect to business," he said. "After U.S. Steel took over the facility and I was not retained, Bob and Al helped me through the tough times and worked with me to find employment.

"Over the years, I was fortunate to be promoted to vice president and then president. The owners allowed us to operate the business without any interference but would offer any assistance when needed."

Nolfi said he felt the reason that Camp-Hill was so successful was due to the family atmosphere the owners created and the business model they introduced at Camp-Hill.

"The bonus plan allowed all the personnel to be included in the company's success by paying bonus every six months. Along with the family picnics every year, these two perks truly made everyone feel part of the organization."

Patsie's 'black book' didn't have phone numbers; it was filled with financials

While Patsie loved to get his hands dirty, he didn't have the same passion for the company financials. All he wanted to know was the bottom line: Am I making money?

Karen Trautwein recalled: "He didn't want to know any other details. I almost had to sit on him to keep from spending money. "I'd say, 'Come on, you can't spend it this month; wait.'"

Al Hillegass also recalled a time when Patsie wanted to buy a half-million-dollar crane for the Hill-Camp plant: "I was sitting in Patsie's office, and he was telling me about a crane he wanted to buy. 'What do you think of that?' he asked. I said, 'What do you do with that?' 'Well, we'll do jobs with it, or we'll lease it out, you know?' he said. 'I'm going to buy it.'"

"Well, if you think that's a good idea, go ahead," Hillegass said.

Patsie called Bobby Campana, who was managing the company financials at this point.

"He reached Bobby and said, "We want to buy this, Bobby.' 'How are we going to buy it, Dad?' Bobby asked. 'Well, we're going to pay cash,' Patsie said. 'We don't have any cash,' Bobby answered. 'What do you mean, we don't have any cash? Where'd it all go?'"

"Well, Patsie blew up, and Bobby said, 'I'll be right down, Dad.' He showed him the books. 'We're not broke, but we sure can't afford to buy that crane,' Bobby explained. 'We need to be careful with our money.' Bobby then left and Patsie turned to me and said: 'Geez, I'm glad that that came up, and we didn't have to buy the crane.'"

But when it came to a manager asking Patsie to approve a purchase, it was a slightly different story.

Mike Marsico recalled how Patsie kept a black book showing company financial balances: "If I ever went and asked, 'I need this; can I buy it?' Patsie would open a desk drawer and pulled out a little black book. He looked in the book and said, 'Yeah, go for it' or 'Hold off.' He really tried to know where every penny was.

"But he never portrayed that. He never let people know that he had this money. To them, he wanted to be seen as just an everyday Joe."

Karen Trautwein recalls that Patsie, at night when nobody was in the office, would go through the files to see what was going on. Essentially,

CHAPTER 14

he pretended he had no idea what was going on and what the company's current financial situation was at any given moment.

"When he talked to you the next day, he already knew the answer, but wanted to make sure you got the right answer," she said.

Patsie threw unforgettable Christmas parties

To show how much he appreciated his customers, Patsie hosted what many consider to be "legendary" Christmas parties. They were held in venues such as Tom's Country Place in Avon. Often, as many as 400 people attended.

Patsie often put his daughter, Patti, in charge of the menu and decorating. He had her buy Capodimonte porcelain favors for the women, four-in-a-pack cigarette favors for the men, and live evergreen decorations from greenhouses. Music was always provided by live bands.

Patsie realized it was all part of doing business. It was his way to say thank-you to all the customers—especially the many steel plant clients—that made the company so successful.

Patsie used to remind his workers that you always should knock on the door to the party with your feet because your hands are filled with gifts.

Unfortunately, rules and regulations now don't allow the freedom of past gift-giving, so Christmas parties aren't what they used to be.

A homemade go-kart showed the kids they had a great dad

Patsie loved his children—and what better way to show that love than by building them a go-kart? Interest in gasoline, miniature vehicles was booming, and Patsie set out to build one for his kids, primarily David (who was about 9 at the time).

The Campanas were living in Weirton, West Virginia, and Patsie used his lunch hours to assemble the go-kart in the Patterson-Emerson Comstock back shop. He built it from scratch: welding tubular steel together and adding wheels, a seat, and a gasoline engine.

David, Patti and Pat Jr. check out the go-kart Patsie built.

When Patsie brought it home, the kids realized that not only did they have a go-kart (which nobody else around them had), they also had one cool dad.

Patsie even painted No. 8 on the car, the number of the 1956 Indianapolis 500 winner. The amazing little car was fast; it could reach 35 mph. Unfortunately, David crashed it the second time he drove it, and the kids were saddened to see it all bent up and damaged.

David is sent to college with a warning

When it was time for Patsie to send his first-born child, David, to college in 1966, he took out a $4,500 loan for tuition, drove to John Carroll University, unpacked the car, and didn't mince any words.

"Well, see you later. We're going to go have lunch. Don't come home until Thanksgiving, and don't flunk out of school because I don't want you going to Vietnam," he warned.

David moved into the dormitory, passing all the other mothers and fathers who were crying because their little one was going off to college. But there was no such scene for him. He got his orders from Patsie, and he followed them: he didn't flunk out, and he didn't get sent to the Vietnam War. Despite having to participate for two years in Reserve Officers Training Corps in college, David was deferred from military service following a hunting injury—a fellow hunter accidentally shot David in the foot.

CHAPTER 14

Patti Ann was always Daddy's girl

Patsie, like many dads, developed a special relationship with his daughter. He never raised his voice with Patti Ann—probably because she seldom got in much trouble. As a result, it was a completely different treatment than what her brothers received.

Nearly every weekend, Patsie would take David and Patti to their grandparents' house. The visit was a way for Patsie to demonstrate respect for his parents so the children would learn likewise. The children saw his respect and love for his parents—and it made an impact.

When Patti worked at the company, Patsie often dropped by her desk and chatted about life and family. And, lucky for both of them, nobody would interrupt the boss and his daughter—they could talk as long as they wanted.

Not even family members were immune from being fired

One of the most difficult challenges for a family business is having to fire a family member. Patsie was not afraid of the task; he could fire his children multiple times and not bat an eye.

Italians, by nature, are said to be passionate people. While their anger may rise to a high point very quickly, it can subside just as suddenly, and forgiveness follows right on its heels. This is how Patsie operated. When he saw an injustice or infraction, he responded. He held people accountable to do the right thing—always.

Mike Marsico, now the company's COO, was among the unfortunate to bear the brunt of Patsie's anger.

"He fired me just once. But he brought me back and gave me a raise," he said. "Some people said, 'I like getting fired. I come back and get a raise.'"

Marsico remembers one time that David Campana and Pat Campana Jr. were both fired on the same day. Even Patti was terminated once, following a spat with a fellow employee.

One particular incident of Patsie's quick temper had an unexpected ripple effect. At the Campana office on West Park Drive, the space on the second floor was shared by the company attorney, Dick Colella.

Colella had a client meeting in his office: a widow who was discussing her late husband's estate.

Suddenly, over the PA system came Patsie's booming voice: "David, this is your father. Get your ass in my office, now!"

David had done something to anger Patsie, and Colella's client heard the off-color PA announcement.

Colella made the best of the situation and talked to Patsie.

"Pat, it's time for me to move," he told him.

Patsie, sounding contrite, replied, "Yeah, I know; I shouldn't've done that. Well, I'll help you find a place; let's go look for something right now."

"The fortunate thing about that particular situation was that Patsie knew this widow very well," Colella said. "He and her husband had been very close friends. Thank God it was her."

Colella ended up moving his office to a separate building, and the relationship survived the test.

An angry Patsie is trumped by his father

It was sometime in the late 1950s or early 1960s, and Thomas and Maria Campana held a weekly spaghetti dinner at the tavern for the family, as they had for years. All the cousins and their parents were there, so many people that the tavern's pool tables were covered with boards so everyone had a place to eat.

Later in the evening, folks went outside to the garden area where the grapevines grew and the children were playing.

Patsie saw Pat Jr., then about four years old, misbehave. He didn't like it. Patsie grabbed Pat Jr., intending to express his disappointment. All of a sudden, Thomas's hand came down on Patsie's arm.

He said, "You leave him alone."

Thomas didn't have to ask Patsie twice. If there is one emotion that is carried through the generations in Italian families it is respect for elders. The matter ended there.

CHAPTER 14

Rich Colella figures out the anger/cool-off thing

Rich Colella, an attorney and son of Campana attorney Dick Colella, was hired by the company to assist with the Texas-based properties. At the time, he was based in Dallas.

Working with Patsie was a bit of an eye-opening experience.

"He didn't have professional parents, he wasn't sent off to a fancy college, and he didn't have a plan already laid out for him," he said. "He just kind of had to do everything himself, so he always struck me as being much more direct and honest than a lot of the clients I had been used to dealing with, which was good.

"It's a little bit—not scary—but a little shocking sometimes. He was a very passionate, emotional guy. And for me, I had never really had anybody yell at me professionally or whatever, and it took me a while to realize that, well, that was just how he operated.

"He could go from being angry with you one minute to the next minute, that feeling was gone, and we were on to the next thing."

Colella said it wasn't anything personal or long-lasting; it was just how he would express frustration.

"It was a big educational process."

In his experiences with Patsie, Colella learned that being assertive can lead to success; just going along with the group did not always work.

"What I tended to learn from Patsie is that sometimes going with the flow just isn't enough to address a certain situation or be successful in a certain context," he said. "Sometimes you've just got to grab the bull by the horns and get it done whether you knock a few things over or tick off a few people.

"As long as you're doing what you think is right and you're passionate about it, there's a path to success there. It's helped me during my career, too, being more assertive about things and speaking my mind, sometimes a little more than was comfortable."

Death of his brother Larry hits Patsie hard

Patsie had not experienced the death of a close family member until his younger brother Larry was killed in World War II.

The two brothers parted after an argument in May 1943, when Larry enlisted in the Army. Patsie was furious Larry had signed up because he was worried he might be killed. The two never spoke to each other again after the argument; Patsie eventually enlisted in the Navy.

Some three months after D-Day, Larry was killed in France.

Patsie, 23 at the time, had not even been at sea one month. He was heartbroken and spent an extended time in sick bay to deal with his grief.

Private Lawrence Dino was killed September 1, 1944, he was only 21 years old. He had been serving as a driver for a general when he was shot by enemy fire. He received the Purple Heart posthumously.

Larry is buried at The Brittany American Cemetery, St. James Manche, France. In 1959 when Patsie was working in Italy, he visited Larry's gravesite, cried on his knees and made peace with his brother.

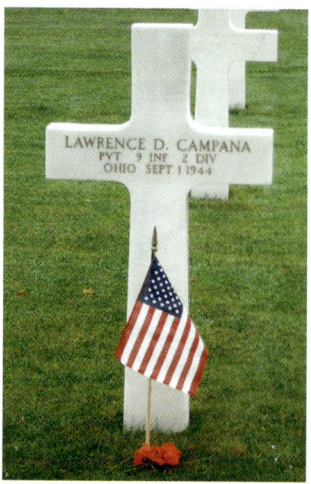

Larry Campana is buried in France.

Patsie's love for cars and planes provided many memories

Like many teenage boys, Patsie loved cars and couldn't wait to get his driver's license. After he earned it, it was off to the races—in a vehicle

CHAPTER 14

with no seat belts. Once, he was taking his brother Baldo and sister Rosemary for a ride, and he wasn't sparing the horsepower.

Patsie flew around the neighborhood in a convertible. Rosemary was in the back seat. But when he got home, Rosemary wasn't there. Patsie had zoomed around a corner, and, somehow, Rosemary had fallen out of the car. Patsie backtracked and found Rosemary sitting on the curb with her elbows on her knees, waiting for him to come back.

The incident had no impact on Patsie's taste for flashy, fast cars. He bought a new 1978 Corvette to zoom around town, and that sporty number so impressed Larry and Pat Jr. that when they opened a Quaker Steak and Lube restaurant in Sheffield Village years later, they purchased an identical Corvette to display there.

Also in the Campana garage was a black Cadillac Sedan de Ville, which Patsie purchased from company foreman Jake Strickler. This car became one of his favorites.

But the auto that people remember most is the 1981 DeLorean—the type that was the time-travel vehicle in the movie "Back to the Future." Patsie was one of the first in Ohio to purchase a DeLorean.

The DeLorean had a futuristic design, with trademark gull-wing doors. Patsie had lots of problems with the car, including being locked inside six times. The dealership had to send out a technician to open the door or sometimes Patsie just broke a window to exit. Nevertheless, Patsie loved the DeLorean, though he eventually sold it. One of the main reasons he liked the DeLorean was because it looked like it could fly; so, it was only a matter of time before Patsie owned his own aircraft.

In the late 1980s, when Camp-Hill purchased Delta Tubular Processing in Houston, Texas, it became clear to Patsie he would need an aircraft for traveling. He acquired an Aerostar twin-engine aircraft, but it wasn't long before he stepped up to a business jet.

With a pilot and co-pilot on the payroll, Patsie was living his dream. His Camp-Hill partner, Al Hillegass, recalled that Patsie would spare no expense for travel when the pair went to Texas.

"We would go down to Delta or Bellville and Patsie would say, 'We can fly there; I'll pick you up in Pittsburgh,'" Hillegass said. "I said, 'No, you don't have to pick me up; I'll get a commercial plane or whatever. It's out of your way to come here.'"

Patsie wouldn't have it. "Well, maybe you can come here and fly with me," he said, and Hillegass declined to do that as well. "But it was kind of cute," Hillegass said. "I kept telling him, 'Patsie, you know, this is a great expense. I don't know why you're doing this.' He said, 'Because I want to. I want to have my own plane. Look, that's what I want to do. That's me; I want to be able to pick up the phone, tell the pilot I want to go somewhere, go to the airport and go.'"

A 1981 DeLorean.

Sister Rosemary was there to lean on

As Patsie's only sister, Rosemary Campana Hribar, was the baby of the family and was very special to Patsie. After he settled his family in Lorain, his job still took him out of town throughout the week. Rosemary, living a little more than a block away, spent a lot of time with Jeneé and the children. Patsie really appreciated this, and it made him happy that she and Jeneé were as close as sisters.

As time went on and Patsie decided to start his own company, he often reflected on how Rosemary took on the responsibilities of her mother Maria, whose health was declining. Patsie could not have taken the huge business leap with a clear conscience had Rosemary not graciously and lovingly intervened. He made sure she knew how much he appreciated her and asked Scotti and David to carry out the wishes he had for Rosemary in the event of his death, which they did.

Patsie was close to his mother Maria and visited her often when he was in town. He would take her for car rides, bringing along Rosemary's two daughters, Maria and Andrea, with his brother Scotti and Marc, his first grandchild.

And, of course, the rides weren't complete without a special treat: stopping at Maria's favorites—Amy Joy Donuts and Arby's.

Patsie liked to fly, but he didn't like to swim

None of the Campana children remember being in the water with Patsie; he didn't swim after his war experiences.

While a swimming pool was a popular item at the Lorain Country Club, as well as the kids' homes when they moved into their own houses, Patsie never went in.

Once, when he was asked why, he paused for a moment before answering, very quietly, "Because it reminds me of my days in the Navy."

Obviously, being in the water would trigger unpleasant memories of the war, and he wanted to avoid reliving them. One can only imagine how some of those experiences affected him emotionally.

The Pinewood Derby gives Patsie an opportunity to teach honesty

When Larry Campana was about 8, he wanted to join the Cub Scouts. Jeneé decided she would do her part and be a den mother. Patsie, likewise, helped Larry with scouting activities. And, when it came to the Pinewood Derby, he taught Larry an important lesson in life.

The Pinewood Derby brought together fathers and sons to build a wooden race car. They would then enter the car to compete in the annual derby. A kit is purchased from a hobby store, and the scout follows instructions closely, but can shape the wooden block and paint it as he sees fit. The race car is supposed to be the work of the scout, and the father offers advice and guidance.

So, Larry worked on his pinewood racer for four and a half weeks.

Patsie resisted the urge to build it for him, just offering his input now and then. When father and son went to the competition in Lorain, there were some 600 Cub Scouts there.

Larry was very proud of his racer. However, he took it out of its shoebox home, looked around, and his face fell. Patsie asked him, "Why are you so bummed out?" "Dad, my little car doesn't look anything like some of these other guys' cars," Larry admitted.

Patsie said, "Well, that's probably because they didn't make it, son, like you did. Their fathers probably put it on a lathe and cheated."

Patsie became a little upset and approached the Scout director.

"I thought this was for the Cub Scout to make this. How could he make something that looks like he turned it on a lathe?" he asked the official.

"Well, I guess you don't know what it's all about around here," the director said.

Disgusted with how the official dismissed the challenge, Patsie said to his son, "You know, Lar, I don't think you want to be a Cub Scout anymore."

Larry said, "Dad, if that's what you think, that's fine."

He learned an important lesson from his dad. Rather than pout about incident, he turned his interests to sports, such as wrestling and baseball, and excelled in them instead.

Putting the kids to work as soon as they could

When you own a family business, usually all family members are expected to pitch in—including the children, as soon as they are old enough.

Patsie, with six children, was never at a loss for helpers. He had young Pat Jr. help him pick up scraps of electrical wire that were left from his jobs. After collecting them for about six months, there was enough to strip or burn the coverings off the wire. Then they took the copper to a recycler and sold it for scrap.

Being a child of the Depression, Patsie valued what could be reused or recycled. He also used the rubber treads from old tires to resole his shoes. He was one of those people driven to find different uses for things. He'd make his own furniture out of aluminum angle metal and side it with redwood cedar planks. He saw the value of sturdy construction and knew its strength because he made it himself.

The Campana brothers: Scott, Boby, Pat Jr., Larry and David.

When his son Larry was a teenager, Patsie would bring home drawings of the estimates that had to be done—at the time, he was still working for Hatfield Electric while building his own company on the side. He used to pay Larry $1 per page to do all the estimates.

Patsie called Larry the best estimator he ever had, but then Larry found out that he was paying his men $30 a page. In response to Larry's indignation, Patsie said Larry, at the age of 12 or 13, was able to complete them faster than any of his men did.

Patsie paid his children in experience. He didn't believe in an easy ride for any of them. Nothing was ever just handed to them, and the children developed a good work ethic. He was a patient teacher, but that didn't extend to overlooking a miscue by someone who had been trained and was being careless—a reprimand would then be unavoidable.

Patsie, the boxing fan

Patsie was a big boxing fan. He frequently watched matches on TV while decked out in boxing shorts, shoes, and socks. He often went to his son Scotti's house to watch.

Patsie and Scotti.

Once, Scotti, also a passionate boxing fan, got a call that said he had better come to the house right away because, in advance of an important Mike Tyson fight, Patsie was about to pull out his tooth because it was giving him such pain. He numbed the area with Anbesol (an oral anesthetic) and whiskey, grabbed it with pliers and a screwdriver for leverage, and pulled the tooth out. Once the operation was over and things had calmed down, Patsie and Scotti took off to Scotti's place to watch the Tyson fight.

Patsie was that tough. His dentist, Dr. John Brletic, told the family at Patsie's funeral, "Your dad was amazing. I've been a dentist for a while. He came to me for his dental implants, and he did the operation without Novocain. I've never seen anything like it."

Billy Carter and the inaugural "beer party"

When Jimmy Carter was running for president in 1976, Leo Koury spearheaded the efforts to convince Lorain County to support Carter. Patsie, Koury's best friend, joined in.

Carter won, and when he was inaugurated in January 1977, Patsie hosted a "beer party" at the Washington Hilton for the Lorain County contingent that attended the inauguration. The guest of honor was Billy Carter, the popular, beer-guzzling brother of President Carter.

There was one slight problem: Patsie was serving Michelob, which was gaining ground as an upscale-type beer. Billy, however, preferred Pabst Blue Ribbon, a lager for those with plebian tastes.

CHAPTER 14

Patsie and Billy Carter at an inauguration party for Jimmy Carter.

Jimmy Carter with Patsie and Jeneé.

A shipment of Pabst Blue Ribbon was ordered for Billy, and the party got into full swing when it arrived. Billy was happy.

Speaking Italian in Italy

When Patsie was on one of his vacations to Italy, he was accompanied by his attorneys, Dick Colella and Ray Miraldi. All three can trace their heritage to the same region in Italy: Abruzzo. Patsie's parents were from Barrea and the families of Colella and Miraldi were from Montenero, a short distance away in the Apennine Mountains.

Patsie was fluent in Italian, but with a heavy Abruzzi accent. Colella was fluent in Italian at the time, but having studied two years of Italian at a university, he spoke a more grammatically correct version than Patsie. This discrepancy created some humorous incidents when Patsie and Colella were abroad. Patsie would get very angry when they were in Italy if people didn't understand him because of his dialect.

So, when the three went to Italy, they decided that, just for kicks, the minute they boarded the airplane they would speak nothing but Italian. But Miraldi wasn't very fluent, so the ruse only lasted about a day, and that was the end of that.

But it was still fun, and they all joked that had their parents not migrated to the United States, they would probably be tending sheep in the hills of the Apennine Mountains.

The Metropolitan: Patsie's venture into the newspaper world
In the 1980s, Patsie became angry with the local daily newspaper, The (Lorain) Morning Journal. He was tired of reading only negative news about a town that had so many good things happening. Patsie loved his town and the people in it and decided to take action. In response, on the third floor of his East 28th Street office building, he and his son David started a publication called The Metropolitan.

At the time, Patsie had grown unhappy with newspapers in general. So the duo put together a free weekly newspaper focused on business news and distributed it directly to homes.

"There was a lot of stuff in it that was good," said Mike Marsico.

Despite this, because the issues were free, the newspaper had to be supported by advertising. It made a go of it for 10 issues, then it was discontinued because The Morning Journal was putting pressure on businesses that were advertising in both publications to choose the Journal only.

Welding while dressed in a suit
One memory that many family members and friends share is how Patsie was prone to give welding lessons—no matter what he was wearing: a

welding suit or a business suit. As a result, many of his suits and sports coats had holes from burning cinders.

There once was a time, soon after he had opened his West Park Drive office, when the family was all dressed up for a wedding.

At that moment, the company was focusing on cast iron welding because of a partnership with Egon Evertz of Germany. In the car on the way to the wedding, Patsie told Jeneé he needed to stop by the office to make sure the workers were welding the cast iron correctly—there was a big job under contract.

Patsie was wearing a welding mask and his dress suit. Everyone got out of the car to watch.

Patsie told the welder, "No, no, no; not like that. Give me that electrode."

He grabbed the welding electrode out of his hand and, wearing a welding mask and a dress suit, showed the men how he wanted it done. The sparks flew everywhere, but Patsie wouldn't leave until he saw that the welders were using the correct method—then the family could go to the wedding.

Not really a religious type of guy, but...

Patsie was not what you would consider a religious type, but he had a solid foundation to rely upon, growing up with his mother being a devout Catholic. There was, of course, church every Sunday as he grew up and a shrine in the living room for his brother Larry, who died in World War II. Patsie was used to meeting nuns in the family from Rome who came to visit, and took pride in that distant cousin Santina Campana was being considered for sainthood.

Although Patsie did not talk about God often and frequently did not attend church in his later years, he knew in his head that God was there. He asked for God's guidance and believed that his life was blessed. Under glass on his desk, Patsie kept a prayer written in his own handwriting that was important to him. He often said it gave him guidance to be the man that he was.

Here is the prayer:

> *Holy Spirit, you who solve all problems, light all roads so that I can obtain my goals.*
>
> *And you who give me the divine gift, forgive and forget all evil against me and who in all incidents of my life are with me, I want in this short prayer to thank you for all things as you confirm once again that I never want to be separated from you.*
>
> *In spite of all material illusions, I wish to be with you in eternal glory. Thank you for your mercy towards me and mine.*

EPILOGUE

Patsie Campana, a self-made man who lived the American Dream, raised a wonderful family, and left a powerful legacy when he died. He always took the opportunity to share an observation, lesson, or piece of advice. Some of his favorites:

>**On business:** "Don't be a big hog; be a little pig because big hogs get slaughtered, and little pigs just keep eating."
>
>**On smoking and foul air:** "You know, if you stuck me in the clean air of Colorado, I'd probably die."
>
>**On being humble:** "I want to be like an iceberg, where only a little bit of me shows."
>
>**On failure:** "No, no, we're just not succeeding at the rate we figured we were going to succeed, but we will."
>
>**On difficulties:** "We don't have problems; we have opportunities."
>
>**On his success:** "Not too bad for a guy who flunked the first grade."
>
>**On leaving a mark:** "If a man is to have an accomplishment of any kind, he must leave something behind."

Of his family: "This is what my life is all about. My wife and my kids come above everything else. These are my loves. After that comes my work."

Those adages were deep in meaning, but so were the many comments Patsie drew from business and personal friends throughout his life:

"We don't have the same background, but we are almost the same mold. We both started from nothing, we both work hard, and we both are now trying to bring our sons along in the business. But let me say I don't belong in Patsie's league. He is strictly an asset in Lorain."
— Carl Gumina, building contractor from Avon, 1973

"I'm sorry to learn that your mother passed away. She must have been a wonderful person to have left a legacy like you. Whatever you do, however high you climb, you will always be what your mother created. And I think you are special."
— Irving Leibowitz, editor, The Lorain Journal, 1975

"Just a note to commend you for your purchase of the former Koehring facilities in Lorain. When Koehring pulled out, it left a serious employment gap in Lorain, and I'm delighted that you are moving to fill the gap. That shows real civic-mindedness on your part!"
— Rep. Donald J. Pease, U.S. House of Representatives, 1978

"God Bless You, Patsie!! We love you for helping make Lorain greater and saying such positive things!
— Joe Calta, Lorain City Schools superintendent, and his wife Ruth, 1979

"It is the unanimous choice of our convention committee that you honor us by being our main speaker at our evening banquet. You may select any subject; naturally, we Italians are proud of the fantastic progress

EPILOGUE

you have made in our community, and you can probably give us some anecdotes that led to an outstanding Italian American in our community."
— Anthony J. Murello, convention chairman,
Lorain Italian-American Veterans Post, 1979

"I had the pleasure of knowing Patsie C. Campana from the day he approached our bank almost two decades ago to start his own business... He had a genius about him to solve major problems for the steel industry, as shown by his many patents.

He served as a member of our Board of Directors for 13 years. During this time, he was a valued member of our board. His expertise in business matter was a great help for our board and management of the bank. Patsie represented the real spirit of the free enterprise system of our country; starting in mid-life to form his own company and being able to realize the American Dream for himself, his wife and his family."
— Stanley G. Pijor, chairman and CEO,
Lorain National Bank, 1995

"Patsie Campana became one of the most creative and innovative suppliers of goods and services—always developing products and services that were aimed to lowering costs and improving quality. His many contributions are too numerous but two stand out: his process to weld cast iron and his cored wire system for making ladle additions to molten steel....

During his business career, if you came to him with a problem in iron and steel making, he would innovatively and diligently work on a viable solution... His company was one of the major tributaries to the mainstream of iron and steel making."
— A.L. Hillegass, former Camp-Hill partner
and U.S. Steel vice president, 1995

"Patsie Campana demonstrated a unique and thoroughly effective ability to innovate, research, develop and take to market a wide range

of products and services to the steel, construction and related industries, both domestic and foreign, while at the same time providing overall control, management and leadership of a rapidly developing group of successful and profitable companies.

He was a tireless 'hands-on' CEO who devoted much of his time working to advance the interests of his companies. He was an 'on-the-job' executive who lived for business.... Despite a lack of formal education, he demonstrated a unique ability to act with remarkable effectiveness in directing all aspects of the businesses."

— Dick Colella, attorney, 1995

To describe a husband or father, it may be unfair to be asked to use one word. But these thoughts from the family speak volumes:

Love—
"Oh, my God, he loved his family. Oh, my God. He loved his family as much as I love all my kids. He just couldn't control himself, he loved them so much."

— Jeneé Campana, Patsie's wife for 47 years

Dynamo—
"He was amazing. He was like a dynamo. He never, never stopped. When I was a little boy, he worked constantly. He'd be working 12-hour days, I remember."

— David Campana

Non-judgmental—
"My father taught me never to judge another person, because we do not know what their circumstances are. This was one of many things that have helped guide me in my life. I was so blessed that he was my dad.'"

— Patti Campana-Manetta

EPILOGUE

Giving—
"He always gave much more than he took. It was never about him. He was like the little Keebler elf in the background, making all the cookies so everyone else could enjoy."

— Larry Campana

Respect—
"When my dad spoke, I listened, and he had my full attention. I learned when I was young not to let my mind wander when he was talking, because he could tell. And if a thought was in his head, right or wrong, and that was his way, that's the way we were going to do it."

— Pat Campana Jr.

Hope—
"Here's a story about a couple who got married, traveled all over the country just to keep moving his career along, and my dad boldly said, 'OK, at the age of 48 with six kids, I'm going to start my own company.' It's a story about hope, and hope is what we are promoting now to sustain his legacy."

— Bobby Campana

Extraordinary—
"He was special. He had a sparkle in his eye; you could be mad at him, and you'd see him smile at you, and that'd be it. You could be in a room with your back to him, and you knew he was there. He could change your life, not just with money; he could change it with a word."

— Scotti Campana

IN CLOSING

He represented a 'bright light' that can be attainable to everyone. We hope that you are inspired by his passion for life and for learning. We hope that you take away the knowledge, knowing that dreams are certainly possible with enough focus, hard work and determination. We hope that you take away his love and respect for his fellow man at every level of society. Let you 'light' burn brightly and continue to encourage our young people to have a hunger for learning and a curiosity for life. Each of us have our own unique gifts and our 'light' will make way to inspire future generations!